the
healing
energies
of
light

the
healing
energies
of
light

Roger Coghill

Gaia Books

A GAIA ORIGINAL

Books from Gaia celebrate the vision of Gaia, the self-sustaining living Earth, and seek to help its readers live in greater personal and planetary harmony.

Editor	Jinny Johnson
Designer	Sara Mathews
Picture Editor	Kathy Lockley
Managing Editor	Pip Morgan
Production	Lyn Kirby
Direction	Joss Pearson, Patrick Nugent

® This is a Registered Trade Mark of Gaia Books

Copyright © 2005 Gaia Books
an imprint of Octopus Publishing Group
2-4 Heron Quays, London, E14 4JP

Distributed in the United States and Canada by
Sterling Publishing Inc.,
387 Park Avenue South, New York, NY 10016–8810

Text copyright © 2000 Roger Coghill

First published in the United Kingdom in 2000 by Gaia Books

ISBN 1-85675-223-2
EAN 9 781856 752237

A catalogue record of this book is available from the British Library.

Printed in China

10 9 8 7 6 5 4 3 2 1

Disclaimer
The author of this book is not a physician, and the ideas, procedures and suggestions in this book are intended to supplement, not replace, the medical and legal advice of trained professionals. All matters regarding your health require medical supervision. Consult your medical practitioner before adopting the suggestions in this book, as well as about any condition that may require diagnosis or medical attention. The author and publisher of this book are not responsible in any manner whatsoever for any injury that may occur directly or indirectly from use of this book.

Author's note

For the physicist, light is part of the electromagnetic spectrum whose energies continually surround and penetrate all living beings, a spectrum which stretches from the powerline frequencies near one end to X-rays near the other. Light is special: it connects all material things. Yet if we mark it on the electromagnetic spectrum it occupies an area that is very small, but the only part of the entire spectrum which humans can overtly sense. For the biologist, it is light which gives plants the energy to convert carbon dioxide into glucose and release the oxygen which gives us life. It is light which gives us a window on to the real world. That same light also nourishes the souls of humanity: without proper light plants grow pale and people grow sad.

So light extends its influence into the very depths of our being: without it we would fall melancholic and our souls would languish. No, more than that – we would not even be able to draw breath. Hence all life comes from light, and it lifts up our spirit to joyfulness.

In previous books I have explored most other parts of the electromagnetic spectrum, but somehow I have left the optical frequencies - light - until last, and I would not even then have thought of writing this book unless prompted by Gaia. I am glad the publishers per-suaded me! Now having completed the work, I realize the impossibility of placing all there is to say about the healing energies of light between two covers. The reader should regard my efforts as only a summary of the vast subject of light and its healing effects.

The topic is hugely exciting and, like some infant lying in a cradle, scarcely gives any inkling of the mature adult it is destined to be. With light therapy, we stand on the edge of extraordinary new developments in medicine. I hope I have helped the reader to take a timorous first look into this new world.

R W Coghill

Roger Coghill

Contents

Introduction
The glory of light

8–13

Chapter 1
Sacred light

14–41

Chapter 2
Light cycles and life cycles

42–65

Chapter 3
The nature of light

66–89

Chapter 4
The power of sunlight

90–125

Chapter 5
Healing with light

126–149

Bibliography   150

References   151

Resources   153

Index   156

Acknowledgements   159

Introduction: The glory of light

As you enter Chartres Cathedral, France, in the cool semidarkness, with the murmur of the Litany in the background, the sensation of antiquity is so overpowering that you feel that you may have entered the 12th, rather than the 21st century. As your eyes become accustomed to the gloom, tall pillars of the great nave emerge, like ghostly giant sentinels. But there is a feeling of something else, of an enriched, blue-tinged light.

Your curiosity is aroused by this strange sensation and you peer around in the twilight, searching for its source. Perhaps, on the way to Chartres, the sight of the incandescent sunflower fields, stretching endlessly yellow across the plain towards a sundrenched horizon, under a cloudless summer sky, has affected your vision?

Then, looking upward, you see the origin of the blueness, and gasp. They tower there, enormous bejewelled windows of the most intense azure, illuminating each of the millions of visitors to this magical cathedral over the last thousand years. These, among the oldest stained glass windows in Europe, create an unforgettable image of light, bathing the innermost soul. Small wonder, in an age when printed books had not been invented, that pilgrims felt the healing energies of being bathed in that deep blue light as if from the very Tree of Jesse itself.

The windows of Chartres (left) are called the eyes of France. Medieval manufacture of painted glass, the so-called stained glass, was shrouded in so much mystery that all sorts of fables attended the process. The famous blue of the glass in Chartres is said to have been obtained by grinding down sapphires, and the deep red by mixing in pure gold. In fact, copper was used to obtain red; the blue was probably made from cobalt.

Nevertheless, the setting of that great cathedral is a very fitting introduction to a book on the healing energies of light. An early medieval catechism of the bishopric of Treguier, Côtes du Nord, France asks what should one do on entering a church? The answer is clear and firm: take holy water, pray to the Almighty, then wander around the church and look at the stained glass. The monks of Treguier must have known that this procedure could instill a healing effect.

Light's secrets

Light is everywhere, but its essence cannot be seen and, as the prism illustrates, it holds many secrets. One secret is a kind of conjuring. For what human beings see with their eyes is not quite as simple as one might imagine. Throughout the ages different people have brought a different understanding to what they see, cladding the images with their own experience and that of their primeval instinct. When the natives of the continent of America encountered the Spanish explorers for the first time, they could not "see" the ships that brought them because they had no visual concept of galleons. The way our brains interpret the light falling on our eyes is flavoured by our individual experience.

The Sun and its light has no history, only a character. It has always been there and always will be, and its influence on life will be discussed at length later in this book. The Sun has featured in virtually all the religions and calendars known: from Stonehenge's hele stone, where sunlight touches a stone said to heal illness, via worship of Egyptian, Incan and Mayan sun-gods to the beliefs of today. The Gospel according to St John opens with a clear exposition of the light of life: the light which shines in darkness, the light "which lighteth every man that cometh into the world".

Not all light is sunlight or the light from other suns. It can originate from fire, from electricity, and even from the creatures of our planet. Anywhere there is energy, there is likely to be light, if we define light as the visible part of the electromagnetic spectrum. Scientists would agree that every energetic action produces an electric field, a field of electrons, and this field can be transduced into the frequency of light, as photons jump from one shell around an atom to the next.

The light of fire was said to have been stolen from the Gods of Olympus by Prometheus, who gave it to humans, but then paid the penalty of being chained to a rock for eternity. Huddled in caverns very different from Chartres, our first forebears used fire to dispel the darkness of their caves and to create heat for their cooking. For most of us, light and heat have been inseparable ever since.

Endogenous light

The discovery and investigation of the endogenous organic light given off by every living being is still, at this beginning of the Aquarian Age, unfolding, though there are distinct signs that the ancients were also aware of it. Experiments at our own laboratory show that endogenous "light" can be disturbed by other electromagnetic fields, with consequent adverse effects, and it is this endogenous light that needs protection if we are to remain healthy. The therapies central to this book show that the body and its energies can be rebalanced by the use of light. I believe that light therapy will play a vital role in the medicine of the 21st century.

Sacred light

Light is holy. There can scarcely be any religion ever contemplated or followed which does not place light at its centre. Light is generally used as a symbol of life and spirituality, while darkness is seen as representing the forces of evil and death.

Today, despite all our technology, we still have a reverence for light and an awareness that its mysteries remain unravelled. Scientists continue to argue about the nature of light – whether its established speed can be exceeded, if it is particulate or wave-like, and if there may, after all, be an ether for light to traverse. They are still discovering new qualities, new facets, new applications. The compact disc uses laser light to engrave and read information at the speed of light, but this is already obsolete technology in the world of information storage. In the future we shall increasingly be using light in the form of fibre optics to communicate faster than ever before.

But light has also come to mean the link between the inner workings of humans and the world about them, a sanctified practical bridge with the real world. It has crept into our thinking and our language in innumerable ways: to "see the light" means to understand, to become "enlightened"; "hiding one's light under a bushel" means to disguise true intelligence.

Light brings richness to our experience, sharpness to our observations, and illuminates the depths of our souls. Turner's painting *The Angel Standing in the Sun* (left) is a perfect example of the spiritual power of light. The Sun's rays enliven us and lift our spirits. Each dawn gives us renewed hope, new determination, and a fresh start. Small wonder that light is seen as a symbol of divine power. "Pines and sunlight are stronger than any dream", said Robert Pirsig in his best seller *Zen and the Art of Motorcycle Maintenance*. He recognized intuitively the benefits of our life- and health-giving Sun.

Spiritual light

A circular emanation of light surrounding the head, the halo has been used to depict personal holiness in different religions for more than 2000 years. In Christian art, haloes were used solely in conjunction with Jesus Christ until the fifth century, when they were also applied to saints and to the Virgin Mary.

"The world is charged with the grandeur of God./It will flame out, like shining from shook foil", wrote the poet Gerard Manley Hopkins (1844–89), expressing a spiritual view of light shared by saints, prophets, and poets of different religious traditions through the ages. The attempt to convey the mystery of God or spiritual revelation and the joy it can bring has long challenged the powers of religious writers and artists. And it is perhaps not surprising that most have resorted to radiant light – seemingly the most immaterial of elements – to convey the ineffable splendour of the divine.

In many religions, light is used to represent divine power, or what the German theologian Rudolph Otto called the "numinous", in terms of its most obvious forms in this world – the Sun and its rays, fire, stars, and lightning. And light is not only used to convey mystical experiences, such as the blinding flash St Paul saw on the road to Damascus. In religious ethics, it has also come to represent the forces of good, truth, and righteousness against evil and the "powers of darkness". This aspect is best known from religious art – a softly glowing halo or aura surrounding the head or body is used to indicate sanctity.

Hinduism: light of the gods

The divine power of light has often been described in terms of the Sun – some of the earliest references to which occur in the Rig Veda scriptures of Hinduism. A collection of 1028 hymns dating from about 1300 BCE, the Rig Veda includes ritual praises of various gods. The 19th-century scholar Max Müller suggested that every god mentioned in these hymns was connected with the Sun. But although a number of gods, such as Vishnu and Agni, do have solar attributes, his view never gained acceptance. The god Surya, however, is fully identified with the Sun: he is said to drive a chariot pulled by seven horses, described as brilliant rays of light; the stars "creep off like thieves" as he "the maker of light" appears with his "hair of flame". Also, in the same hymn, Surya is invoked to cure jaundice: the yellow condition of the skin was felt to be analogous to the colour of sunlight and so curable by Surya on homeopathic principles.

Perhaps the most dramatic "eruption" of light in Hindu scriptures occurs in the Bhagavad Gita (c.500 BCE). This classic Sanskrit text describes the spiritual struggles of its hero Arjuna who, at one point, sees the god Krishna – until then disguised as his charioteer – reveal himself in his divine form. The god appears as a "unified multiplicity", with hundreds of eyes staring out from countless faces. Krishna's radiance is so brilliant that it can only be compared to the "light of a thousand suns" – the very image that the nuclear scientist Robert Oppenheimer spontaneously used when he saw the test explosion of the first atomic bomb.

Arjuna is struck with awe and amazement and exclaims that he can see all the gods contained in Krishna and that the god's eyes are like the Sun and Moon, and his face a holy fire giving "light and life" to the universe. Later on, Krishna emphasizes the spiritual significance of light by explaining to Arjuna the three conditions of faith – that people of light will worship gods of light, those whose nature is of fire will revere gods of fire, and people of darkness will pay homage to the spirits of the night.

The most palpable connection with light and fire for modern Hindus comes during Divali, a four- or five-day festival of lights held in the autumn. The word divali derives from *dipavali,* a "row of lights", and refers to the lines of candles, lamps, or electric lights that festoon buildings, balconies, and window ledges at festival time. Light, in this instance, is a potent symbol at different levels: under the practical guise of easing the return of Lakshmi, goddess of wealth and good fortune, it serves to maintain the living flame of life at the onset of darkening winter days. It represents the exultation of the heart in this most important and joyful of Hindu festivals.

The most important element in the Divali celebrations is the worship of Lakshmi, the goddess of wealth and good fortune. Doors and windows of homes are left open to welcome her inside, and the plethora of burning candles ensures she can find her way in the dark.

Light of awakening

The other major faith to originate in India was Buddhism, which was founded by Siddhartha Gautama (c.563–483 BCE). A prince who pursued and reached his enlightenment, he became known as the Buddha – the "Awakened One". As a way of describing revelation, light plays as prominent a part in Buddhism as it does in Hinduism. Buddhist scriptures describe the central idea of nirvana – spiritual enlightenment – less in terms of the dawning light or blinding flash of other spiritual traditions and more as the overcoming of samsara – the changing, decaying world of humanity. In fact, the light which is usually associated with nirvana is a negative one – that emitted by the fires of greed, hatred, and delusion: the word nirvana literally means "extinction" and is best thought of as the blissful state that comes into being when the three fires have run their course.

But there are important instances of Buddhism's regard for radiant light as a mark of virtue and advanced spirituality. In the scriptures known as the Dhammapada – a collection of spiritual sayings compiled in the third century BCE – it is said that those who are virtuous "shine a long distance away, like the Himalayas", whereas the wicked remain in darkness "like arrows thrown in the night". Another section, on being a monk, says of a young mendicant who follows the way of the Buddha that his "light shines bright over the world, like the brightness of a Moon free from clouds". Elsewhere, the radiance that comes with being fully "awake" – by reaching Buddhahood – is emphasized by a series of contrasts which involve the natural and human worlds: "The Sun shines by day, the Moon by night. Clad in armour, the warrior shines, as the Brahmin priest shines while meditating. The Buddha, however, shines day and night – in his radiant splendour shines the man who is awake."

Some of the most intense descriptions of spiritual light in Buddhism come in the person of Amida or Amitabha ("Infinite Light"). A godlike, celestial Buddha, Amida is the

A stylized flame of light rises from the head of this medieval statue of the Buddha from Cambodia (above). The flame represents the supreme wisdom that Prince Siddhartha Gautama gained at his enlighten-ment, when he became the Buddha, or "Awakened One". Swirling gilt scrollwork creates the effect of sacred light around this Buddha figure from Thailand (opposite).

central figure of the Pure Land school, which evolved in
Japan during the 12th and 13th centuries. He is said to pre-
side over a paradisal sphere or realm known as the Pure Land.
His body – which is of a height and brilliance beyond the
imagination – gives off a golden glow as he sits on a lotus
flower emanating light. His form is encircled by an enormous
aureole or halo, and he bears 84,000 marks which are the
physical forms of individual virtues, each of them shooting
out 84,000 beams of light.

Zoroastrianism: light of the fire

The idea of spiritual light lies at the centre of Zoroastrianism
in the form of fire. The Zoroastrian faith began about 3000
years ago in the Middle East. Its founder was the prophet
Zoroaster, or Zarathustra, whose teachings form the religion's
basis. Most Zoroastrians today live in India and are known as
Parsis ("Persians") – a reminder of the fact that their ances-
tors migrated from Iran in the ninth century CE to escape
Muslim oppression. At the heart of Zoroastrianism stands the
one god, Ahura Mazda – a radiant being who wears a gown
of stars and is manifested in the sky as the Sun and on the
Earth as light. Ranged against him is the evil spirit Angra
Mainyu, a powerful adversary who, it is believed, will finally
be overcome by the forces of good.

Fire has a central symbolic role in
the lives of Zoroastrians and is the
focal point of their fire temples,
such as this example at Ateshgan
in Azerbaijan (above).

One of the core ideas of Zarathustra's teachings was that fire
symbolized righteousness, or *Asha*. This meant that hearth
fires, the Sun and also the Moon became important as focal
points in ritual prayer. In modern times, Zoroastrians are
obliged to pray five times a day in front of a source of light,
which may be a special lamp at home or, preferably, the fire
kept alight in a Zoroastrian temple. Some devotees believe
fire is an actual embodiment of the radiant power of god,
while others see it more in symbolic terms – expressing the
undefiled purity of his being. Either way, Zoroastrianism is
one of the few religions to have such a direct manifestation
of light at the centre of worship.

Light of salvation

In the three major religions of the Western world – Judaism, Christianity, and Islam – light is used to convey the form of God, intense spirituality, and virtue. For Jews, the seven-branched candelabra, or menorah, has for many centuries kept the flames of hope burning during periods of darkness – from the destruction of Jerusalem by the Romans in 70 CE to the Holocaust.

The redemptive power of light is most physically evident in the celebration of Hannukah – a winter festival of lights that lasts eight days. Hannukah commemorates the time during the 2nd century BCE when, led by Judas Maccabaeus and his family, the Jews threw off the yoke of their oppressive Syrian-Greek rulers. After their victory, a group of Jews entered the Temple in Jerusalem and found it filthy and desecrated. They also discovered a small jar containing enough oil to light the Temple lamp for one day. By an apparent miracle the lamp kept going for eight days – an event that Jews remember by lighting special eight-branched Hannukah lamps in their homes and in public places.

Light has always been much more than a symbol in Judaism. According to Genesis, the first book of the Bible, light was physically created by God, who is described in terms of light elsewhere. In Exodus 13, for example, Moses encountered the angel of the Lord as a "flame of fire out of the midst of a bush". After Moses led the children of Israel out of Egypt into the wilderness, God appeared to them as a pillar of cloud by day and a "pillar of fire" by night to show them the way. When God communicated with Moses his "glory" was seen in the clouds; and his appearance on Mount Sinai to give Moses the Ten Commandments was preceded by thunder and lightning before he "descended upon it in fire".

Elsewhere in the Bible, Psalm 27:1 states that "The Lord is my light and salvation". And in the Talmud – sacred scriptures compiled by rabbis in the first centuries CE – God's presence

Depicted as a German shepherd, Moses gazes in awe at the sacred flames of God, blazing from within a bush, in this 17th-century coloured engraving by Matthaus the Elder. Moses is shown undoing his shoes because, according to Exodus 3, God commanded him to take off his sandals – "for the place where you are standing is holy ground".

The wondrous colours of stained glass (overleaf) are brought to life by the power of light.

is called the Shekhinah and associated with brilliant light. In a passage about the afterlife, the righteous are said to sit "with their crowns on their heads and bask in the radiance of the Shekhinah".

A connection between light and divinity is also found in the Jewish mystical tradition known as the Kabbalah, which evolved during the Middle Ages, particularly in Spain and France. The classic text of the Kabbalah is called the *Zohar* ("Brightness") – a name derived from a verse of the book of Daniel (12:3) that says "And they that be wise shall shine as the brightness of the firmament; and they that turn many to righteousness [shall shine] as the stars for ever and ever." The *Zohar* refers to God as the *En Sof* – "the Infinite" – who is connected to the world through a series of ten emanations known as the *sefirot*, which together form the divine light of the world. The *Zohar* also says that although divine goodness resides in humans as sparks of light, the effect of evil is to enclose the sparks in "shells". These must be cracked apart before the divine light trapped inside can shine out.

Christianity: light of life

In the Christian tradition there are many instances of light being equated with spiritual power – most notably with Jesus Christ himself. The most explicit references to Christ being the "light" come in the Gospel of John, which is the most mystical and theological of the four gospels. In the first chapter, which describes the mysterious relationship between the Logos – usually translated as "Word" – and God, it is said that in God "was the life; and the life was the light of men. And the light shineth in darkness; and the darkness comprehended it not." These somewhat cryptic phrases set the scene for the appearance of Jesus, who is described as the "true light, which lighteth every man that cometh into the world." Throughout the gospel there is a tension between the divine light of Jesus Christ that enables people to "see" the truth of God and the spiritual darkness of those who reject his message.

A luminous golden halo, expressing divine glory, invariably dominates the icon paintings of the Orthodox Church, as shown by this 17th-century Serbian depiction of Jesus Christ as "Pantocrator", ruler of the universe. Icons were venerated as spiritual objects in themselves and were sometimes believed to possess miraculous powers.

Jesus himself makes this point when healing a man who was born blind (John 9). He ends the episode with a saying that applies to his ministry as a whole: "I am come into this world, that they which see not might see; and that they which see might be made blind". Elsewhere, he declared that he was "the light of the world" and he says that anyone "who followeth me shall not walk in darkness, but shall have the light of life".

In Christian art, Jesus' sanctity is often conveyed by a halo of light. One source of this might have been the radiant form that Jesus is said to have assumed on one occasion during the later stages of his ministry. The gospels say that Jesus led his disciples Peter, John, and James up a mountain to witness an event that became known as the Transfiguration. While the three men watched, Jesus was "transfigured before them…his face did shine as the Sun, and his raiment was white as the light". Jesus is then joined by the forms of Moses and Elijah and the scene reaches a climax with the appearance of a radiant cloud from which the voice of God declares: "This is my beloved Son, in whom I am well pleased; hear ye him."

Elsewhere in the New Testament, the most dramatic instance of the ability of images of light to transform the material into the spiritual comes in the Revelation of John the Theologian. In this, in a vision of the end of time, the new Jerusalem descends from heaven, and John attempts to express the inexpressible: the city, he says, was the "glory of God" and its light shone with the radiance of gemstones; the gold of which the city was made was so pure that it shone like "clear glass"; and its foundations "were garnished with all manner of precious stones", such as jasper, sapphire, emerald, and chalcedony. The 12 gates were made of 12 giant pearls, and the city's street was also "pure gold, as it were transparent glass". So dazzling was the overall effect that John states that the city had no need of the Sun and Moon – "for the glory of God did lighten it, and the Lamb is the light thereof".

Haloed in gold, Jesus is "transfigured" before his awestruck disciples, Peter, James, and John, in this 16th-century Flemish painting. Directly above Jesus is the figure of God, while on either side are Moses and Elijah. The Transfiguration is a momentary revelation of Jesus' glorious divine nature shortly before his crucifixion.

Islam: light of the Prophet

Islam was founded in the early seventh century CE by Muhammad, the Prophet of God. Like the Judeo-Christian tradition, Islam also identifies the one God with light – this is explicitly said in Chapter 24 of the Qur'an, Islam's holy book: "God is the Light of the heavens and the Earth; the likeness of His Light is as a niche wherein is a lamp (the lamp in a glass, the glass as it were a glittering star) kindled from a Blessed Tree, an olive that is neither of the East nor of the West whose oil wellnigh would shine, even if no fire touched it..." (translation by A.J. Arberry). In the passage that follows, the light of God is said to be found in places of worship that he has sanctioned; and unbelievers will be deprived of light and encounter a darkness like that of a "bottomless ocean spread with clashing billows and overcast with clouds".

The identification of God with light naturally appealed to those within the mystical tradition of Islam known as Sufism. For example, the Sufi Jalalu'l-Din Rumi (1207–73) used the image of light as a unifying force to express the view that behind the differences between religions lies the same eternal truth: "The lamps are different, but the light is the same: it comes from beyond."

In the first centuries of Islam there also arose the esoteric idea of Nur Muhammad, "Light of Muhammad" – namely that before God made the universe he formed the Prophet from a "handful of light". This conception was elaborated upon by the tenth-century Muslim scholar al-Masudi, who wrote that before creation God emitted a flaming radiant light from his glorious being and scattered it among invisible atoms, which he then brought together to make the Prophet. Echoes of this doctrine can be found in some of the beliefs of Manicheism, a dualistic religion founded in Iran by a mystic named Mani (c.215-76 CE) In the Manichean account of creation, the Creator was threatened by the principle of evil or darkness and so turned himself into particles of light which he threw into the created world.

In the Muslim faith, the shining, light-reflecting surfaces of domes of mosques symbolize the glory of God. Because figurative dipictions of God are prohibited in Islam, Muslim artists use abstract designs and effects of light to convey the divine. Glazed tiles, painted in azure, colbalt or other shades of blue, create a sense of purity and brilliance (opposite).

Light in mythology

Light also plays a central role in many ancient mythologies. The Phoenician people, for example, worshipped Baal and Moloch, who represented, respectively, the beneficent and the injurious powers of the Sun. Baal Haddad was the young, bellicose god of wind and thunder and some versions of Phoenician mythology suggest that he challenged and then defeated El, the greatest patriarchal god. For this he himself was killed, but was later resurrected by his wife or consort, Anat. He declared war, and won victory over, all the other gods. Despite further challenges to his rule, he was allowed, by decree of El, to rule during the seasons of fertility. He came to be seen as a phallic fertility god (or gods) known as Baal, and the Canaanites celebrated his death, disappearance, and resurrection as part of their annual fertility rituals.

Moloch, or Molech, may have been another name for Baal-Hammon, who was worshipped in cult ceremonies at Tyre and Carthage. Human sacrifices were made to him; some sources even suggest that live children were placed in his outstretched arms, then allowed to fall into a fire below.

Apollo, "the Shining One"

In Ancient Greek mythology, Apollo was one of the twelve great Olympian gods. From Homer's time onwards he was called Phoebus Apollo, "the Shining One", and he later came to be seen as a sun-god, and to be identified with the sun-god Helios. Apollo was born to Leto, daughter of the Titans Coeus and Phoebe, on the island of Delos. The Homeric Hymn to Apollo describes his birth, "...Leto's time was come and she strove to bring forth her child. She clasped her arms around a palm tree, kneeling...while the Earth laughed for joy beneath, and the child leaped forth to the light."

As well as fulfilling his role as the sun-god, Apollo was the god of music, healing, and archery. From birth he proclaimed himself the prophet of Zeus, and he slew the occupant of Delphi, the great serpent Python, in order to found his

Greek sun-god Apollo is depicted perched on his chariot and racing towards the Sun in this 16th-century ceiling fresco (above) by Romano Giulio. The fresco is in the Room of the Sun in the Palazzo del Te in Mantua, Italy.

oracular shrine there. This was the home of the Delphic oracle, which became the most important in Greece. His victory over Python represents the triumph of the god of light over the forces of darkness. Apollo is often depicted in post-classical art, appearing either with his sister Artemis, the archer, or in the role of sun-god, driving his sun-chariot across the broad sweep of the sky.

Re, the sun-god

Ancient Egyptian mythology in all its different versions recognizes Re as the creator, the sun-god, the inventor of kingship, and the first king. Each day he walked through his kingdom, or was seen sailing across the sky in his boat of a million years. To the Egyptians, all kings were sacred because they embodied the image of the sun-god himself. When they died, they were accepted by the gods into the afterlife and triumphed over death, just as the Sun daily triumphed over the darkness of night.

Re, the creator, had many names and forms. He was known variously as Re, Re-Atum, Amon-Re, Re-Horakhty, and the Shining One. In one version of the creation story, darkness covered the watery abyss called Nun, wherein lay the amorphous spirit of the creator. From the darkness, the primeval lotus arose, opened its petals, and revealed a young god seated within its golden heart. Light streamed forth from the divine child's body, and universal darkness was banished. This child was the creator, the sun-god but, just as the lotus closes its petals every evening and vanishes into the waters, so too chaos reigned every night until the god in the lotus returned at daybreak. Because chaos was not permanently vanquished in the beginning, it lived on in the form of serpents always alert to attack the sun-god. This serves as a parallel for the unending war between the forces of chaos and order.

One of Re's daughters was named Hathor. She, too, took many forms, but in her role of the Eye of the Sun she was at her most cruel. She held the power of life and death over all beings, and in her anger none dared oppose her. Although she was protector of the gods, she abandoned Egypt for Nubia after a quarrel with her father. In her absence, darkness and chaos threatened light and order. Without the power of his Eye, Re himself was blind to the tactics of his would-be attackers. Hathor was eventually brought back to Egypt by Thoth, the wisest of all deities. By telling her a series of moral stories or fables, Thoth persuaded her to return to her homeland, and all of Egypt celebrated her return.

Central and South American legends

The powers of the Sun and Moon also feature in South American mythology. The Maya originated around 2600 BCE and their civilization flourished around 250 CE in present-day Guatemala, Belize, Honduras, El Salvador, and the Mexican Yucatan peninsula. From 900 CE, their influence declined, though their peripheral centres were not overthrown until the Spanish conquest of 1541.

Mayan mythology is not yet wholly understood, but we do know that the Maya were highly accurate timekeepers and their calculation of the true solar year was more accurate than the Julian calendar invented by Caesar. Their interest in the various calendars they devised was partly related to their agrarian lifestyle, but the Maya were also astronomers. The astronomer-priests considered the Sun, Moon, Venus, Jupiter, and the other planets to be deities, whose rhythmic dance in the skies could serve as a guide for the conduct of humanity.

Some versions of Mayan cosmology honour Itzamna as the single lord of the heavens, supreme god, and god of the sky. Other versions embrace a pantheon, or host of gods, many with overlapping roles and responsibilities. In this system, the First Mother, the co-creator of the new cosmos, is a moon-goddess. Another figure, Ix Chel, or Lady Rainbow, is also identified as a moon-goddess .

The great Aztec calendar stone (above), made in 1479, was designed to represent the Aztec universe. At its centre is the face of the sun-god, Tonatiuh, and surrounding him are four cartouches giving the dates of the previous ages of the world. In the next circle are the names of the 20 days in an Aztec month and around them are designs symbolizing the Sun's rays.

In Mesoamerica the earliest deities were the jaguar gods. The Mayan sun-god Kinich Ahua traces the Sun's path across the sky, but at night when the Sun enters the West door and falls into the underworld, he becomes a fearsome jaguar god. The maize god, another important figure in the pantheon, is also associated with the themes of life and death. He is linked to the sun-god, following the solar cycle of sky-travel, descent, rebirth, and return to the sky-world.

The Aztecs, or Mexica, were an ancient civilization whose gods demanded frequent sacrifices in the form of human hearts flung from the steps of their temple-pyramids. Under their leader Montezuma I they established a bloody and turbulent empire in central Mexico.

Their sun-god had many aspects. The Mexica believed that the Sun itself was formed by the self-sacrifice of the ugly deity Nanautzin, who threw himself into a fire and was transformed into the Sun. The deity Tecciztecatl, who had meant to jump with him, hesitated and later became the Moon, a masculine figure ever after associated with cowardliness. The intriguingly named Tlazolteotl, or "Goddess of filthy things", was also considered to be a moon-goddess. Tonatiuh was the sun-god, symbolized by a solar disc. The Mexica also used a special altar to the Sun for their coronation rites, and they sacrificed slaves as part of the ritual. Warriors had a special devotion to Tonatiuh, who was also called "He who goes forth shining".

Other aspects of the sun-god are Tlalchitonatiuh, known as the "groundward sun", sometimes illustrated as being slain by the evening star and swallowed to become Yacomicqui, the sun "killed" or sacrificed by night. Yohualtonatiuh is the "night sun" that dwells in the underworld as a wrinkled and ugly being. Because night was associated with ugliness and the underworld, most Mexica shunned the night, and only brave, trained priests dared venture forth after dark.

North American legends

The central role of the Sun in indigenous people's cultures features in Native American legends from the numerous tribes of the United States and Canada. Several of the tribes, including the Cheyenne, Sioux, and Pawnee performed the traditional ceremony of the Sun Dance. This involved a number of men dancing for three or four days and nights, while being watched by their fellow tribespeople and having blessings conferred on them by shamans. The ceremony also demanded fasting and self-mutilation by piercing the skin with skewers. The following Cherokee legend offers an explanation of why the Indian people danced to the Sun.

The Sun detested the people of Earth because when they looked up at her they squinted and screwed up their faces, but they smiled at her brother the Moon. This made her very jealous and she sent down a fever to kill the people. The fever was so successful that the remaining few people on Earth resolved to kill the Sun, for they feared extinction. By means of magical powers, they turned a person into a rattlesnake and sent it to lie in wait for the Sun outside her daughter's house. By accident, the snake attacked the daughter, not the Sun, and she died soon afterwards.

When the Sun discovered what had happened, she shut herself away and grieved. Now the land was free from fever, but the people were cold and dark. So they sent seven chosen people to the land of ghosts to bring back the daughter of the Sun. As her ghost danced past them, the people struck her down and trapped her in a box. On the journey back, the daughter complained that she could not breathe, so they opened the lid just a little. Out flew the daughter, now transformed into a red bird, straight back to the land of ghosts. Seeing the people return empty-handed, the Sun began to cry, and her tears formed a great flood. To stop the flooding and amuse the Sun, the people of Earth began to dance, and thus they dance to the Sun to this day.

Participants in the Native American Sun Dance gazed fixedly at the Sun while dancing as well as the blowing of eagle-bone whistles. Ceremonial dances (opposite) declined in importance during the first half of the 20th century. But in the 1970s, they were reinstated as a means of preserving Indian identity and culture.

Marking the Sun's light

Much of the architecture remaining from the world's ancient cultures has clear links to solar, lunar, or planetary movements – movements of light. The ancient sites of Newgrange in Ireland, Stonehenge in England, the Menhirs at Carnac in France, the Great Pyramid of Egypt, the step pyramids of South America, and many others were constructed in order to mark the light of the Sun at important times and solstices.

One example is Teotihuacan, which stands close to present-day Mexico City. This now ruined and partially reconstructed city belonged to an ancient civilization that formed Mexico's first great urban society. At the height of its influence and expansion from the time of the birth of Christ to 605 CE, Teotihuacan was almost certainly the largest and by far the most impressive city of pre-Hispanic America. Beyond a doubt is the importance of the Sun and Moon to the earliest inhabitants. The pyramid of the Sun is Mexico's largest pyramid, apart from the ruin at Cholula. It is aligned precisely to allow the Sun to fall directly over the pyramid at noon on two days of the year, 19 May and 25 July.

The builders of Castle Rigg in Cumbria in northern England found a site with a convenient horizon for the exact axis of the setting Sun on the summer solstice. This is the key axis of the year, for it marks the turning point of the light power of the Sun, and is expressed as the farthest point of the setting Sun along the horizon. The winter solstice is of equal importance but less easily visible.

Almost all pre-industrial societies linked the celestial bodies' movements to health, and enshrined this in their temple architecture. In trying to unravel the connections between massive pre-historic structures and their purpose, a number of speculations come to mind. For example, the Sun radiates and so heats stone. Different crystalline stones will excite and release the electrons they contain, and all electrons are by nature negatively charged. Inevitably, therefore, structures such

The pyramid of the Sun at Teotihuacan (above) is one of Mexico's largest pyramids and is precisely aligned so that the Sun falls directly overhead at noon on two days of the year, 19 May and 25 July. The layout of the entire city is based on this alignment. At the heart of the pyramid lies a cave – an inner sanctuary and possibly the reason for the city's foundation.

as Stonehenge, when heated by sunlight, are generators of negative ions, and negative ions are proven to be beneficial to health. Perhaps that is why the wall at Newgrange is clad in quartz, and why the original sides of the Great Pyramid were polished – this increases the production of negative ions. The ancients may have understood the importance of negative ionization far better than us.

The Great Cairn at Newgrange is constructed with a quartz wall face, which is designed to mark the winter solstice. As the weak sunlight of the solstice beams down, the rays pass down a narrow shaft into the cairn's interior. The meaning of this careful, massive architecture is explored in enormous detail by Michael Poynder in his book *Pi in the Sky*, which explores the ancient, traditional Celtic wisdom. Could the spirals carved on the stones at the Great Cairn symbolize some lost technology? What long forgotten message are they giving us? Poynder argues that the great civilizations of the past, including the Egyptian, the Mayan, and the Inca, all fell apart suddenly due to sharp decreases in the life force itself – the energy of the Sun arriving at the planet through the solar wind and interacting through light with our atmospheric densities. At such times, the Earth's own geomagnetic field increases strongly, he suggests, depleting natural fertility and causing an imbalance in the life force.

The curious triple spirals seen at Newgrange are found all over the ancient prehistoric world: in the rock etchings of the Zunis of New Mexico, and on vases from mounds in the Mississippi valley. The same triple spirals were also a favourite design of Bronze Age man in Europe.

These feats of construction in the ancient world, such as the Pyramids and Stonehenge, are still inexplicable and imply unexpectedly advanced technologies. One calculation esti-mates that the whole of the then known population of the British Isles would have had to be at work for seven years to

Newgrange (above) in County Meath, Ireland, was built around 3200 BCE and is one of the oldest structures in the world. Its Gaelic name means "cave of the sun".

raise the sarcen circle and central trilithons at Stonehenge. Why was it worth such a massive effort? The importance of agriculture to the ancients may provide a clue.

Sunspot cycles

A significant correlation between the crop production levels of common vegetables with the sunspot cycle, was reported in the journal *Nature* in 1974 by King, Hurst and colleagues from the Appleton Laboratory, England. Sunspots are areas on the Sun's surface that are cooler than their surroundings and have a particularly strong magnetic field. They come and go in a regular cycle of about 11 years. King discovered that the best crop years always occur at the peak of the sunspot cycle. Could it be that Stonehenge was not simply a Sun calendar, useful in itself for farmers, but was also used to monitor sunspots, or rather, their magnetic storms? If so, it could also have been used to predict the likely pandemics of influenza and a host of other disruptions associated with sunspots. Sunspots cannot be counted without telescopic apparatus, but there is another way of predicting them by measuring temperature changes and comparing these with records of previous years, as the research was able to show.

One way of monitoring temperature without a mercury glass is to measure the length of a long metal bar. But it would need to be anchored at one end by means of a heavy weight, and that weight should not expand along with the bar. The heavy stones of Stonehenge would have fulfilled that role admirably. A rise of only a fraction of a degree would cause a 100-metre (330-foot) rod to expand by 12 centimetres (nearly 5 inches), quite enough to monitor the sunspot cycle. Silica, by contrast, would expand only a hundredth of that distance for the same temperature change. During the course of time, however, the iron would oxidize into non-existence, leaving the stones behind. I admit this is speculation, but it would not surprise me if the ancients used some method of this type to follow the effects of the sunspot cycle on Earth.

Stonehenge (opposite) stands on Salisbury Plain in Wiltshire in the south of England. The oldest parts date from about 3100 to 2300 BCE. Experts believe that not only were the stones precisely placed to align with the movements of the Sun but also that they could be used to predict events such as eclipses.

Sculptor of light

Californian artist James Turrell is a sculptor like no other –
his subject is light. Turrell works with light, not as painted on
canvas or even computer screen, but using the large natural
space of open air. He aims to open our eyes to light and to
bring the sky into our lives.

Many of his works are simple white rooms with geometric,
sharp-edged holes in the roof. The effect of the holes is to
bring the sky to the viewer and frame its colours in a totally
unique fashion. In one installation in the Newlyn Gallery in
Cornwall, Turrell has created what seems to be a room without light. As the eyes become accustomed to it, the darkness
turns to a thick grey and a black rectangle that seems to
come from nowhere, appears on one wall. On approaching
the rectangle the viewer finds it is a hole, a space – not a
painting. The effect is dramatic and illusory: one woman
tried, unsuccessfully, to sue Turrell when she broke her wrist
at one of his exhibitions. She leaned against what she thought
was a blue wall and found that it was nothing but light.

Turrell's technique forces attention on the quality of light,
just as a framed oil painting does. He argues that many great
painters such as Giotto and Vermeer have taken light as the
real focus of their work, using relatively unimportant subjects.
He points out that in Monet's paintings of haystacks light is
the subject, and the haystack, an inglorious object, is just the
holder of it.

The most spectacular work, and the pinnacle of Turrell's
career, is his ongoing project in the Arizona desert, where
25 years ago he acquired an extinct volcano. In the perfect
cone of the volcano he has carved ten huge chambers linked
by blacked-out corridors. Each chamber has its own skyspace,
the orientation of which has been minutely planned to cap-
ture light from particular features of the night sky. When it is
completed Turrell's Arizona volcano will be an extraordinary
mixture of observatory and sculpture.

On a hillside in Cornwall in
southwest England, James Turrell
constructed a work he calls the
Elliptic Ecliptic. It was part of
a celebration of the solar
eclipse, visible in that part
of the world in August 1999.
The visitor lies inside the
structure, gazes up through
the eye-shaped opening
and experiences a whole
new vision of light
and sky (opposite).

Meditation with light

Light is an important aid to meditation and can increase its effectiveness. In fine weather, meditate outdoors if you can and gain the benefits of exposure to the healing powers of natural light and fresh air, as well as calming your spirit. The important ingredients for this type of meditation are the direct radiation of sunlight at a time other than the midday peak, and either no noise (difficult in these days of motor-ways and aircraft) or some naturally occurring soft sound, such as birdsong, a breeze through leafy trees, or flowing water. A sunlit clearing in a hilltop wood would be my first choice, or a spot near a fast-flowing stream. Parks are also suitable and generally quiet in the late afternoon, which is the best time of day for sunlight meditation. In 30 minutes you should synthesize enough vitamin D for the day, as well as the other useful components of the rays.

Most of these conditions can be achieved only in the warmth of summer. On vacation, reserve the later part of the day if you plan meditation on the beach, and try to sit near a large sundrenched granite or volcanic rock so that you can almost feel its heat. This may not seem a practical option since other beach-users will be intruding on your space, but persevere and you may find places that are worth trying. Wander off from the crowd and explore: you will stumble on a secret place sooner or later!

Collect a nosegay of favourite places for meditation and, while you are in any of these places, take a keen look at the surroundings and store the details in your memory. Later, just by closing your eyes and mentally revisiting the scene, you will achieve the same effect in your mind. As the poet John Donne wrote: "If I perceive I have thee, then I have thee; for all reality is but perception".

A refinement is to watch the ever-changing pattern of light cast by the Sun on the ground, originated by the waving leaves of trees or by the march of clouds. Alternatively, try gazing at a crystal hung in an appropriate position so that its brilliantly coloured prismatic hues catch your eye indirectly.

Winter meditation is not so easy, but you can use a candle or flickering firelight as a substitute for sunlight. Even a ticking clock in a quiet, well-lit room is better than nothing. You may like to play some soothing music, but do leave some time for silence: the wrong music could entrain your mind just when it needs to be quiet.

When meditating indoors, use a negative ionizer to improve the air quality in the room. Negative ions are beneficial for health, but they are depleted by electrical equipment. An ionizer can replace them and give a feeling of wellbeing. Ionizers come in various shapes, sizes and designs, some rather ingenious. I like the design which has its needles on a pointed spike enabling them to turn under the propulsive force of the ions. These are not usually very powerful, but as an adjunct to meditation they have a charm of their own.

Of course, a fine place for meditation is in a large church, illuminated by the rich colours of some great stained glass window. Such places often have lighted candles, and the contemplation of their unwavering or gently flickering flame is a also form of meditation with light.

The physical position of the body itself while meditating is also important. Each hand position of the Buddha had a specific meaning for good reason. In public places, simply sitting normally is a working solution; if you have more privacy you may prefer to lie down. I hesitate to recommend the lotus or similar positions because for some of us that may be painful, when comfort is the aim.

In the final analysis, the best advice for meditation is simply to do it, and you will find "the still small voice of calm". Sunlight and the quiet sounds of Nature will do the rest.

The flickering, dancing light from a burning candle is conducive to gentle meditation, helping to calm the overactive mind and soothe the troubled spirit.

Light cycles and life cycles

Light is fundamental to life. Every living thing on this planet responds to the rhythms of light and dark occasioned by the movements of the Earth. Life is a creature of habit – the habit of responding to light. The Sun, the provider of light, is the powerhouse of life itself – without it, plants could not grow and animals, in turn, could not survive. It is the photo-system of plants that converts carbon dioxide into sugar and provides the world with life-giving, energy-synthesizing oxygen.

We can live without food for a month, survive without water for a few days, but without oxygen we cannot live more than six minutes. We may eat about two kilograms (more than four pounds) of food a day, and drink two litres (four pints) of fluid, but we breathe three and a half kilograms (seven and a half pounds) of oxygen, more than both food and fluid, each day. And all that oxygen, the means of life, comes from the Sun's radiation.

Life on Earth is bound to rhythms of light – rhythms of night and day and changing daylength – caused by the movements of our planet. Every 24 hours the Earth rotates once on its axis, creating the rhythm of day and night. Nearly all living things are linked to this daily cycle of 24 hours. Although most humans no longer live by the Sun – going to bed at sunset and rising at dawn – our bodies still have powerful daily, or circadian, cycles. More than a hundred of our bodily functions rise and fall to a regular rhythm every 24 hours. Blood sugar level, for example, is at its peak in the middle of the day and falls at night. Cells divide at their fastest at midnight and slowest at midday.

There are also annual rhythms of light. The Earth takes a year to orbit the Sun and this, combined with the Earth's tilt on its axis, brings about the seasonal rhythms that affect nearly all animals and plants.

Daily rhythms

Knowledge of the body's daily biological rhythms makes it obvious why jet lag is a problem. When we cross time zones, our daily body rhythms take several days to catch up with our new circumstances, hence the feelings of tiredness and bodily disruption.

This Victorian postcard (opposite) shows a floral clock – a specially planted collection of flowers, which open and close at different times of day. The viewer could tell the approximate time by looking to see which flowers were open

The daily activities of most creatures other than humans are closely tied to the rhythms of light and dark. Diurnal, or day-light-living, animals such as monkeys, apes, and most birds usually find somewhere safe to settle down for the night as darkness falls, and they do not stir again until the dawn. For them, the night is a dangerous time, when the cover of darkness makes it easier for predators to operate. Other creatures seek refuge from the light and emerge only at night. In hot deserts, for instance, the heat is too much for many animals and they prefer to spend the daylight hours in cool burrows and come out to find food at dusk. For amphibians such as frogs and salamanders, which need to keep their skin moist, the drying effects of daylight and sunshine can be too much so they are usually active only at night. Plants show daily rhythms, too. Acacia leaves fold together at the end of the day and the petals of some daisies close as evening comes.

Carolus Linnaeus (1701–80), the botanist who classified the plant kingdom, compiled a floral clock by noting the times different plants opened and closed. In 19th-century Europe such information was used to design formal gardens planted to form a clock face, with flowers in each bed opening at a different hour. What mysterious mechanisms drive these differences is still not understood, but it may have something to do with electromagnetic energy and the specific frequencies it can deliver, rather than simply temperature.

There is clearly more to these daily rhythms than just the plain following of external clues. Experiments show that organisms possess some sort of internal body clock, which is set to a cycle of approximately 24 hours. If an animal is kept in controlled conditions in complete darkness, its normal activity rhythms continue at first, although after a few days they begin to drift slightly from the solar time outside the laboratory. In normal circumstances, an organism's body rhythms are entrained by the environment, generally the changing light levels of dawn and dusk.

Eclipse of the Sun

There is no more startling evidence of the effects on Nature of changes in light and dark than a total eclipse of the Sun. During the brief period of semi- or total darkness at totality, birds fall silent and head for their roosts, sheep cease their bleating, cows stop mooing, and an eerie silence falls over the land, until the eclipse passes and the Sun comes out from behind the Moon once again.

A total eclipse of the Sun happens when the Moon passes between the Sun and the Earth, hiding its light from our view. Although the Sun is at least 400 times the size of the Moon, it seems much the same size because, by a strange coincidence, it is about 400 times farther away from Earth. An eclipse occurs about once every 18 months, but each one is visible only from a small band of the Earth, never wider than about 270 kilometres (167 miles). Outside this, a partial eclipse is visible – the Moon seems to cover just part of the Sun. Astronomers can predict when an eclipse will happen and where it will be visible.

Solar eclipses have always been viewed as awe-inspiring, almost magical events. This watercolour (above) shows a group of Jesuits observing an eclipse in Siam (present-day Thailand) in 1688.

As the eclipse begins, the Moon slowly starts to move over the Sun's surface. It may take about an hour to cover it completely. At totality, when the Sun's face is covered, darkness falls and all that can be seen of the Sun is the brilliant shining corona – the Sun's outer atmosphere. I have measured the geomagnetic field during an eclipse and found that it fell noticeably during that period. During the time of total darkness birds and animals act as though night is falling. Totality lasts a maximum of seven and half minutes, often much less, then life gradually returns to normal.

The diamond ring effect (opposite) occurs just before or after totality in a solar eclipse, when all but a fragment of the solar disc is hidden behind the Moon. The solar corona is visible as a thin, but incredibly bright, ring.

Lunar eclipse

An eclipse of the Moon takes place when the Earth comes between the Sun and the Moon, and Earth's shadow, cast by the Sun, covers all or part of the Moon's face. Unlike a solar eclipse, which is visible from only a small part of the Earth, lunar eclipses can generally be seen over most of the world.

Changing daylength

Plants and animals are also governed by annual rhythms of changing daylength. At the equator there are 12 hours of daylight and 12 hours of darkness all year round, but elsewhere the number of hours of daylight changes to a regular pattern. During autumn in the northern hemisphere, the days gradually shorten until the shortest day on 22 December. They then lengthen again until the longest day on 22 June. The farther from the equator, the greater is the variation between shortest and longest day, until within the Arctic and Antarctic circles there is the extreme situation of constant darkness in winter and constant daylight in summer.

The entraining mechanism for the internal clocks of animals and plants appears to be daylength. It is changing daylength that enables animals to organize their annual activities such as breeding, migration, and hibernation. Climate may change – one September may be much warmer than other; a spring may be unseasonably cold – but the length of a certain day in any particular place will be the same each year. This is a cue that is impossible to disrupt.

As the days shorten, birds such as swallows know it is time to start on their annual migration to warmer climates. For many creatures, the lengthening days of spring are a signal to start their courtship and nest-building activities. The flowering of most plants is triggered by a certain number of hours of

The vibrant sunflower gets its name from its resemblance to the Sun and its radiant beams. Its scientific name is *Helianthus*, from the Greek *helios*, meaning sun, and *anthos*, flower. The sunflower originated in Mexico and Peru, where it was much revered. In Aztec temples, priestesses wore crowns of sunflowers and carried them in their hands.

daylight. Dahlias and chrysanthemums are among the many plants that flower once the days start to shorten – a poinsettia flowers when the daylight hours fall to fewer than 12.5. Other plants burst into bloom with the lengthening days of spring. The spinach plant, for example, flowers when daylength reaches about 13 hours. Some plants, though, do not appear to follow the daylength cues and they flower irrespective of the number of daylight hours. These include sunflowers and tomatoes.

An advantage of using the changes in daylength as a cue to behaviour patterns is that they enable living things to syn-chronize their activities. All the hedgehogs in an area, for instance, will be getting ready to breed at the same time. And if plants of a species flower together, there is more chance of successful pollination. The daylength cue also helps animals and plants to time their activities for the best chance of success and to produce their young and seed at the most favourable time for survival.

In polar regions, the coming of light is a signal for a burst of activity as plants and animals begin a frenetic rush to repro-duce before the return of darkness, for with the the darkness comes dormancy. In the tropics there is little need of such scheduling, since conditions there are favourable year-round and plants and animals can reproduce at any time.

The darkening days of autumn are the signal for many birds, such as Canada geese (below) to start their long migration. Canada geese spend the summer months in northern North America and Europe, but fly south to winter in a gentler climate.

The wonder molecule

How do organisms pick up these daylength clues? In plants, it is the leaves that recognize daylength changes and set chemical processes in motion that enable the plant to produce flowers. In vertebrate animals, the secret of the body's response to light lies in the brain in a gland called the pineal – so called because it resembles a pine cone in shape.

The pineal can regulate seasonal breeding because it has the unique ability to detect the one reliable indicator of the seasons: the number of hours between dusk and dawn. While temperature, humidity, and sunshine itself vary irrespective of season, the hours of darkness are determined solely by the spin of the Earth. It is assumed that the pineal gland uses the visible light frequency for this detection though it is not proven, and the trigger could be some other part of the electromagnetic spectrum (see page 66). The pineal responds to changing light levels to regulate the body's rhythms and produce a hormone called melatonin. Darkness is a signal to the body to produce more melatonin, which prepares the body for sleep – lowering the heart rate and level of alertness, for example. In the morning when light once again enters the eye, melatonin production stops. Obviously in the short days of midwinter melatonin levels will be higher, hence our tendency to feel less energetic.

Pineal gland

Known as the "third eye" by many ancient civilizations, the pineal has long gone unrecognized by science. But now the function and importance of this, the body's natural light meter, is fully recognized. It is known to affect every part of the body's functions, such as reproduction, growth, mood. It may also have an impact on longevity via the release of melatonin, which does much more than encourage sleepiness.

For more than 30 years Russel Reiter, who works at his laboratory in San Antonio's Health Science Center at the University of Texas, has been interested in melatonin, and he

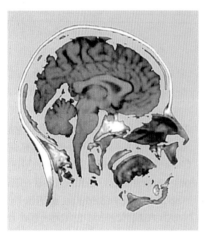

The pineal (pink spot above) is located between the two cerebral hemispheres of the brain.

The illustration (opposite) from a book by René Descartes published in 1662, shows his ideas about the pineal gland (H). He believed that images were relayed from the eyes to the pineal and the reaction of the pineal determined the motor action.

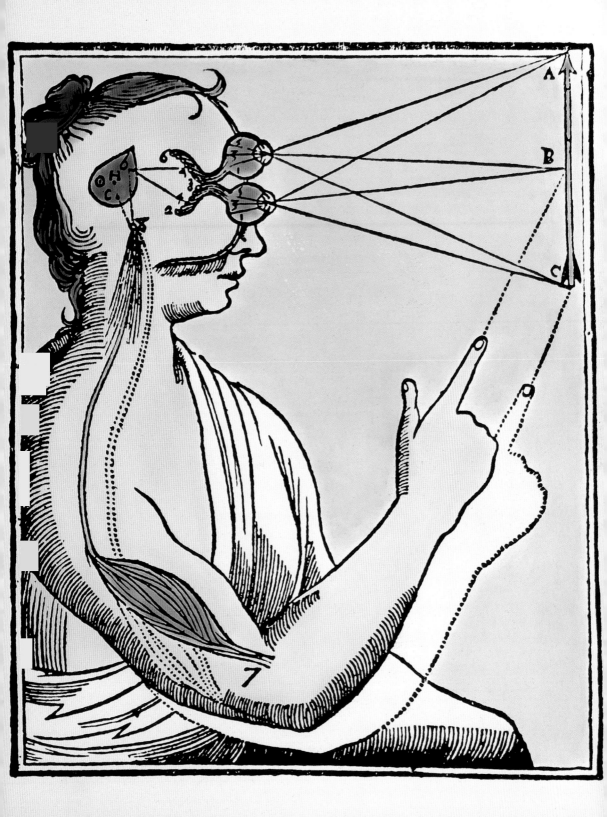

is now acknowledged as the world expert. In the 1960s Reiter and another scientist, Roger Hoffman, identified the role of melatonin in seasonal breeding in animals and put the pineal on the physiological map. To prove its effect they conducted an experiment with male hamsters, a group of which had their pineal glands removed – their pineals are no larger than the period at the end of this sentence. After the animals had been confined for a month in darkness, the testes of those which had had their pineals removed remained normal, while the gonads of their intact companions had shrivelled significantly – they had reacted to the absence of light.

Though melatonin is produced only at night, at least four studies have shown that it is also necessary to receive a good deal of sun during the day for optimum melatonin synthesis. Premenstrual syndrome, or PMS, is one of the many conditions that has been linked with low melatonin levels. One study by Barbara Parry of the University of California at San Diego found that when women with PMS are exposed to two hours of bright artificial light during the day, they make more melatonin at night and their symptoms greatly improve. Astonishingly the 2000-year-old Chinese Tao Tsang text says much the same thing: "exposing the eyes to direct sunlight greatly benefits the brain by stimulating excretions of vital essences there".

Key to cycles of light and life

So melatonin appears to be the key to some of the most important cycles of light and life. How does it work? The pineal gland is connected neurally to a part of the brain exactly above the optic chiasma, the spot where the optic nerve crosses over on its way to the occipital lobes at the back of the head, where information from our eyes is processed. This suprachiasmatic nucleus (SCN) senses these optic signals and relays their passage directly to the pineal buried deep in the brain. (The SCN itself can be damaged by a chemical called glutamate, often used in food additives.)

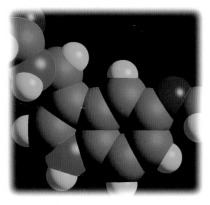

Melatonin, shown above as a molecular model, is the hormone that controls our bodily rhythms such as sleeping and waking and may influence reproductive functions. It is also a powerful antioxidant, protecting the body from harmful free radicals.

The effect of bright light at night, however, is to depress the level of melatonin. This was proved in 1980 by Alfred Lewy, from the Oregon Health Sciences University, a leader in the field of light therapy, when he demonstrated that night-time exposure to very bright light causes a fall in the synthesis of melatonin in humans.

As a molecule, melatonin is deceptively simple, but it has a dual role. As well as regulating the sleep/wake cycle, it acts as an impressive antioxidant and free radical scavenger, picking up stray, unwanted electrons from the body's tissues. Free radicals are emerging as the primary cause of cell damage, as freed electrons desperately try to lock on to any other place for the sake of stability, causing great damage to existing cell processes. The free radical theory of aging has at last become acceptable, and in 1995 scientist Denham Harman gained a Nobel Prize nomination for his work on the subject.

Free radicals

One of the most compelling demonstrations of the effect of free radicals on the length of life was provided by Rajindar Sohal at Southern Methodist University, Dallas. He used two groups of house flies for his experiment – the flies in the first group were normal while those in the second had their wings removed. The normal flies, which could fly, lived a maximum of 28 days. But the wingless flies, which could only crawl, lived an amazing 65 days, more than twice the normal time. This was because the wingless flies consumed less oxygen, resulting in the generation of fewer oxygen-based free radicals. The lowering of their production of free radicals preserved cells vital for life.

The two most common antioxidants in our bodies are catalase and superoxide dismutase. The cockroach, perhaps the creature most capable of withstanding radiation, even in a nuclear reactor, has been found to have incredible supplies of these two enzymes.

This highly magnified photomicrograph shows the sister hormone of melatonin, serotonin, which the body produces in the daytime. The body uses serotonin to make melatonin and serotonin also functions as a neurotransmitter. The task of neurotransmitters is to carry nerve impulses across the minute gap between a nerve cell and a target cell.

How is melatonin produced in the body? Curiously it is made by the action of certain enzymes on its sister molecule serotonin, the hormone that is made during daytime, levels of which can be raised by light therapy. The first of the complicated synthesis steps is from tryptophan, an amino-acid which is ingested in food. Hydroxylase enzymes make use of oxygen and iron to convert this into 5-hydroxytryptophan. This in turn is converted by the dopa decarboxylase enzyme – which needs a phosphorous-containing chemical for its work – into serotonin (5-hydroxytryptamine).

That isn't the end of the story: serotonin is next converted into N-acetylserotonin by an acetylating enzyme, and finally this chemical is converted into melatonin by another enzyme HIOMT (hydroxyindole-o-methyl transferase), which needs calcium for its activity. It is the action of light on HIOMT that regulates the process. Thus the production of melatonin ultimately depends on light and a second messenger, in the form of charged calcium.

Serotonin is a neurotransmitter, the action of which is enhanced by antidepressant drugs. In 1992 a study was published reporting that while light therapy increased the serotonin levels of both normal subjects and those suffering depression, levels in the depressed group increased more. A more natural way, therefore, than drugs to cure depression is simply to get outside into natural light. People who spend a good deal of time outside have few depressive symptoms according to Dr Rachelle Espiritu, a light researcher from San Diego, California.

Protect your melatonin!

Melatonin is precious if you want to sleep well and live a long and happy life. A number of common substances can deplete your melatonin and should be avoided. These include caffeine, as well as alcohol and tobacco. Remember that green (regular) tea is also caffeine heavy, though herbal teas are free

A farmer gathers his sweet-scented lavender crop in the Provençal sunshine (right). Spending time outside in natural light, working or simply enjoying yourself, is the best way to keep your melatonin levels topped up.

from caffeine. Chocolate, particularly dark chocolate with its high percentage of cacao, is a melatonin depleter. There are about 31 milligrams of caffeine in each 45 grams, whereas in milk chocolate there is only 9 milligrams. Colas are also rich in caffeine.

Eating foods that are rich in the amino acid trytophan may help your body to make serotonin, which is transformed into melatonin. Foods rich in trytophan include cheese, eggs, milk, poultry (especially turkey), and tuna.

Other melatonin-depleters are the NSAIDS (non-steroidal, anti-inflammatory, drugs) used for killing pain. These include aspirin, ibuprofen, and indomethacin. Volunteers taking just one dose of aspirin or ibuprofen in the evening suffered a loss of melatonin as high as 75 percent, but the loss from indomethacin was even greater, blocking melatonin synthesis completely. Since melatonin has the capability of reducing hypertension and blood pressure, it could be that NSAIDS, known to increase blood pressure and interfere with anti-hypertensive drugs, act via their effect on melatonin. New research shows that NSAIDS can also damage internal organs.

NSAIDS are so commonly used by arthritis sufferers, usually of middle age or advancing years, and arthritis itself is such a common disorder, that to tell these patients that NSAIDS may not be all good demands that an alternative be offered. First it may be possible to take extra melatonin when the drugs are being administered, according to Bill Sahley at the Pain and Stress Center in San Antonio. He claims that those of his patients who do this report a remarkable reduction in pain. Discuss the idea with your doctor if you are taking these drugs and finding it difficult to sleep.

Beta blockers have been such a boon to those with heart conditions that it is disappointing to discover that these too disrupt the production of melatonin. Beta blockers act on the beta-adrenergic receptors of heart cells, blocking their action and causing the heart to pump less forcefully. However, they also act on the beta-adrenergic cells of the pineal gland. Once more, the answer would seem to be to take additional mela-tonin tablets. The new generation of calcium antagonists (names include bepridil, diltiazam, nicardipine, and verapimil) also block melatonin. Again, a discussion with your doctor about taking supplementary melatonin is advisable.

Other melatonin-lowering drugs include antidepressants such as Valium and Prozac, which may account for their known side effect of causing insomnia. Another depleter is Vitamin B12, taken in great quantity in efforts to relieve stress and increase energy levels. I have mentioned alcohol as a depleter, but paradoxically if taken very late at night alcohol may actually stimulate melatonin production. In a 1994 study by Badia, Murphy and colleagues published in *Sleep Research*, 15 of 18 subjects who drank alcohol at 11 pm revealed significantly higher melatonin levels for the next three hours. Maybe that "nightcap" drink isn't such a bad idea after all.

In some countries melatonin is now available only on pre-scription. It is, however, still freely available and relatively inexpensive at airports and in the USA, and I do not know of any ban on purchasing it indirectly. Alternatively, you can take the herbal remedy St John's Wort (Hypericum), which is a known stimulator of melatonin and has been used as an antidepressant for thousands of years.

The effects of sunlight

There are still many unsolved mysteries about the therapeutic effects of sunlight. We know that it contains a cocktail of radiations and that some, if not all, of these are essential for the photosynthesis of oxygen by plants. The means whereby cyanobacteria, the simplest of lifeforms, do this is easy. They use electrons from water and carbon dioxide, add a dash of light, and turn the elements on the left hand of the formula into oxygen and those on the right into carbohydrates.

This simple reaction probably first made possible all aerobic life on Earth. Later on chloroplasts, special organelles in plants, developed this into a more sophisticated process, with

The benefits of melatonin continue to emerge as discovery piles upon discovery. Many conditions are believed to be alleviated by administering melatonin. These include: age spots, asthma, ageing, AIDS, Alzheimer's, amenorrhea, atherosclerosis, blood clots, brain cancers, breast cancer, chronic pain, depression, diabetes, epilepsy, gastric cancer, heart attacks, impotence, insomnia, irregular menstruation, jet lag, manic depression, melanoma, Parkinson's, rheumatoid arthritis, seasonal affective disorder (SAD), stress, sudden infant death syndrome (SIDS), stroke, and ulcers.

sugar as a by-product. The electrons in the chlorophyll are excited – they gain energy from light – and these can decay either by heat and light (a thermal effect) or by resonance energy transfer (non-thermal), or by successive electron transfers. At this stage of science we do not fully appreciate how resonant effects can also be used to convey very specific biological information. In resonant energy transfer, the electron itself is not transferred, only its vibration, and these vibrations can be frequency or amplitude dependent, just like radio waves.

Chlorophyll itself is a molecule shaped like a tennis racquet, holding a magnesium atom in the centre of what is called a porphyrin ring (the bat), and with a long tail (the handle). The electrons excited in this structure are passed into a one-way photochemical reaction centre, and the excited electrons enter into a second photosystem, where they are transported in a way similar to the process of ATP production in the mitochondria cells, but turned inside out. Plants can thereby make ATP or NADPH, which are needed for the production of carbohydrates from water and carbon dioxide.

Most people today spend their working days indoors. Although many modern office blocks (opposite) do incorporate large areas of glass, allowing people to work in natural light during the day, at night or in dim light they are often lit by fluorescent light. Research has shown that this form of lighting can cause health problems for some people and it also emits higher levels of electromagnetic fields than other light sources.

The sunlight energy required by plants does not, it seems, need to be in the visible light frequency range, and can even be transmitted down a copper wire. In an incredible experiment in the 1930s, a young engineer from the Kansas City Light and Power Company, T. Galen Hieronymus, put a metal plate on a roof exposed to full sunlight. A copper wire was fed from this to the darkness of his cellar and connected to growing seeds in an aluminum-lined box, earthed to the water supply pipework. Similar seeds in other boxes (the control group) were not connected in this way. In the connected boxes, the seeds grew into sturdy green plants, but the unconnected seeds were drooping, with no trace of green. Galen concluded that whatever caused the development of chlorophyll in plants could not be the sunlight itself, but unlike light, was transmissible by wire.

Dark days

Humans, too, need sunlight energy. For some, the effect of the short days of winter can be severe, causing a depressive condition known as seasonal affective disorder, or SAD. During the night the melatonin produced by the body makes us drowsy and helps us sleep. In the morning, when light once again enters the eye, melatonin production stops. But in the dullest days of winter, some people may find that they do not receive enough light to trigger this waking-up process. These people are suffering from sunlight deprivation and can be helped by extra exposure to light during the day to reduce daytime levels of melatonin.

SAD experts advocate a sleep routine with the golden rule of wake up, get up, and if possible get some bright light early in the morning. This has the effect of shifting the circadian rhythm back to a summer schedule, and surprisingly also alleviates SAD. One should also follow the old Greek maxim for understanding yourself: some of us are "morning people" and those who are should try to get the most important tasks of the day done then. For severe sufferers, a specially designed light box, which provides extremely high levels of light, may be the answer (see pages 108–10). Users sit in front of the box for a short period each day. One company has also

invented a natural alarm clock which gradually suffuses the room with light each morning to simulate the dawn, and this too can be of great benefit.

Evening is when SAD strikes hardest. Leave at least an hour after eating before going to bed, reserving that time for an active but undemanding task. Beware of eating more as a result of depression: we all put on weight to some extent during winter, and that extra layer of fat comes in useful against the cold. But SAD sufferers are prone to overindulge, so take care. Regular outdoor exercise, such as walking, is also highly recommended as a way of combating SAD.

People in the Northern hemisphere find SAD is usually worst during February, which is also the peak season for cot deaths. In the Southern hemisphere, July is the SAD season. Choose these times for a winter break, but do not expect it to be a total panacea, since the return to grey skies can bring one down with a bump. It is better to get your sunlight or daylight on a continual basis rather than all at one time. Go out into the daylight at last once a day for say, ten minutes or more. In 30 minutes' exposure to daylight a fair-haired person can generate the vitamin D required for an entire day.

No one likes the dull days of midwinter, but some are more sensitive to the loss of light than others. These sufferers from SAD, or seasonal affective disorder, should take every chance to get outside and get the benefit of what light there is. Even ten minutes a day can make a difference.

The light of the Moon

Cleopatra may have named her son Ptolemy Helios from the Greek word *helios* for Sun, but she called her daughter Ptolemy Selene - the original moonchild - after the second most powerful light in our night sky. The Moon's effect on humans is as well chronicled in history as that of the Sun. Our word "lunatic" comes from the unrest felt by almost everyone on Earth at the time of full Moon. This is no old wives' tale – there is a simple explanation, accepted in astrophysics, for the phenomenon.

The Moon is full when it is on the side of the Earth farthest from the Sun. At that time the Moon comes closest to Earth, drawn inwards by the Sun's gravitational force. In turn, the Moon exerts an influence on the ionosphere, pushing this delicate mantle slightly out of its encircling band around the Earth's atmosphere, and towards the Earth's surface. The ionosphere, as its name implies, is a layer of charged air and particles that envelops the Earth 120 kilometres (75 miles) or so up. The underside of the ionosphere is positively charged.

The ionosphere's positive ions mix with those ions near the negatively charged Earth's surface. The mix of the two is thereby altered, becoming more positive. We breathe in the changed mixture, which enters our bloodstream. This physical change now has a physiological effect. Our blood cells are normally negatively charged, as are the walls of our arteries and veins, ensuring an easy flow as the similar charges repel each other. But when the mix turns more positive as a result of the Moon, the blood becomes "stickier", leading to poorer oxygenation and a resulting increase in psychological stress. At the same time, the white blood cells, which are highly sensitive to electric charges, are also adversely affected.

Lunar cycles

In mental institutions every nurse is made well aware of the personality change of inmates at full Moon. These positive ions also cause an overproduction of serotonin, a stress neuro-

Bats, with their acute hearing and special powers of echolocation, are among the creatures that prefer to live at night – hunting by the light of the Moon rather than the Sun.

hormone and the opposing sister-molecule to melatonin, destroying one's ability to sleep. Robert Becker, a New York doctor and pioneer in bioelectromagnetics research, and his colleagues found that peaks in psychiatric admissions at seven New York State hospitals between 1957 and 1961 coincided with the full Moon, or rather with the electric state of the air. The idea of "dangerous moonlight" is clearly more truthful than the romantics would have us believe. The legends of vampires and werewolves take on a new significance with this scientific discovery.

The energy of the Moon may seem more subtle than that of the Sun, but it is equally predictable, especially for mariners and farmers. Sowing seeds by the new Moon is said to improve their germination. Sunlight is not always the best for embryo health, it would seem. This may be because the Sun's rays are a cocktail, one ingredient of which is an ultraviolet and radioactive component capable of causing mutations.

Does the Moon influence germination? Certainly the legend that it does is ancient: Claudius Ptolemy 2000 years ago wrote: "...[farmers] notice the aspects of the Moon, when at full, in order to direct the copulation of their herds and flocks, and the setting of plants or sowing of seeds; and there is not an individual who considers these precautions as impossible or unprofitable" (*Tetrabiblos* Chapter III).

In 1982, Simon Best, a psychologist, and Nick Kollerstrom, an ecologist, set out the scientific evidence on planting by the Moon's light or in its absence. They stated that whatever requires growth or new development is started during the waxing phase and whatever was needed to dry cure or decrease without decay was performed in the waning phase. Pliny the Elder recommended that produce to be eaten fresh is best harvested at the full Moon, leaving things to be dried until the new Moon. Clearly the Sun's rhythms of light are not the only ones to affect life on Earth.

At full Moon, when the Moon is farthest from the Sun, the ionosphere, part of the upper atmosphere, is "squeezed" towards the Earth. This brings an increase in airborne positive ions at the Earth's surface. These appear to increase aggression and excitement and slow blood circulation in Earth's creatures.

At the time of a new Moon, when the Moon is nearest the Sun, the ionosphere expands, lowering the number of positive ions at the Earth's surface. This encourages plant growth and improves circulation and vigour in animals.

The nature of light

The history of the way scientific thinkers have tried to understand the nature of light parallels the best detective mystery. Throughout the ages, ferocious arguments have raged about what light really is – much of the debate concerns whether light is made up of waves or particles, or both. And along the way, we have discovered the dramatic and unsuspected effects – both beneficial and dangerous – light energies can have on our everyday lives.

What do we mean by light? Most of us think of light as the illumination falling on the world around us – whether from the Sun, an electric source, or a candle – which we can detect with our eyes. Yet visible light is only one tiny part of the vast electromagnetic spectrum of energy permeating the universe. The spectrum ranges from the gamma rays at the incredibly energetic end, through ultraviolet and visible light, to extra-low frequency energy, which powers our homes, factories, and offices.

When we separate light from other parts of the electromagnetic spectrum we are being completely organocentric: in physics, visible light frequencies are simply part of a continuum with the same governing formula. And the only reason we can see light is because we have evolved sensors to do so, which we call eyes.

But what is this light that we see with our eyes? We see light as rays or beams, or as reflections and refractions that fill our world with a wondrous diversity of colour and form. Most of this light comes from the Sun, but whatever its source, light is pure energy. This chapter looks at the basic properties of light and how we detect it. Use it as a springboard for understanding the healing processes described in Chapters Four and Five.

A film of particles

Since time immemorial, human beings have struggled to understand the physical nature of this mysterious thing which enables us to see. Some of the most accurate ideas are many thousands of years old, while some of the most astonishing have only emerged this century!

The ancient seaside town of Abdera on the coast of Thrace now lies in ruins. It is, however, the cradle of Greek thinking which began to explain the intimate nature of light. It was here towards the end of the fifth century BCE that two great philosophers, Democritus and his teacher Leucippus, came up with the idea that all matter is made up of atoms (from the Greek atomos, the word for "uncuttable") and empty space.

No word written by Leucippus has survived, and there are only a few fragments of the writings of Democritus. But their simple idea has survived for millennia, and underscores the nature of light. For these two atomists, sight was the receipt of a physical film of particles.

The Greek philosopher Aristotle was a doctor's son and had a biological approach to science, fuelled by a burning curiosity to understand how life functioned. When it came to light, Aristotle rejected the atomism of Democritus and introduced the idea that light was a psychological aspect of sensation. The Roman philosopher Lucretius, in the first century BCE, tried to restore the concept of light as a physical film formed by particles given off by objects, but he was no match for the reputation of Aristotle.

The crystal-clear light bathing the islands of Greece (opposite) encourages the thought that Aristotle might have been right – light could well be a psychological aspect of sensation.

Aristotle's treatises, or those ascribed to him, describe many things – plants, the locomotion of animals, gravitation, and the physical government of the universe (a best seller in its day, around 300 BCE). Many of his ideas dominated thought throughout Roman times and into the Dark Ages and the Middle Ages. Only with the advent of the Renaissance were his theories questioned and finally superseded.

Splitting white light

The discovery that ordinary light comprised the seven colours of the rainbow (and many more) was first made by French philosopher and scientist René Descartes in 1637. The English mathematician and natural philosopher Isaac Newton, who first saw the daylight that was to make him famous on Christmas Day 1642 at Woolsthorpe in eastern England, refined the discovery. This was that white daylight, shining like shafts into his darkened room, was split by glass prisms into the colours of the spectrum. Newton revealed that white sunlight was a compendium of colours.

We can thank the Great Plague for Newton's groundbreaking work on optics. The plague had closed Cambridge University in 1665, forcing Newton to retire to his mother's farm for two years. What distinguished Newton's work was that he braved new territory by constantly exploring areas outside our senses and our sensations. Between 1665 and 1667 he developed the mathematical technique of calculus and carried out most of his work on the nature and properties of light. He also found time to lay the foundations of the universal mechanics, in which he synthesized the terrestrial science of Galileo with the planetary theory of the German astronomer Johannes Kepler.

Like many scientists before him and since (including Edward Jenner, William Harvey, Galileo, and even, humbly, myself), Newton found that his first scientific thesis was received equivocally when first presented to the Royal Society in London. This lukewarm reception had the effect of holding back his researches until they became massive theses. For example, it delayed publication of his work on light, *The Opticks*, mostly developed in 1666, until 1704. So the document that would forever change the way we understand the properties of light lay dormant for nearly 40 years. By that time the 62-year-old Newton had virtually abandoned his scientific study and had taken up politics as the member of Parliament for Cambridge.

Newton, like Descartes before him, conceived light as being a stream of particles, or corpuscles, that travelled extremely fast in straight lines and created no shadows. Newton used two prisms together and was able to see clearly the difference in the angle of refraction between different colours. When he came to explain it, however, Newton thought variations in the speed of the light determined the order of the refracted colours, while Descartes had thought it was a function of their rotation. Neither proved to be right.

The best explanation had come from Christiaan Huygens, a Dutch physicist who had constructed the first pendulum clock. In 1678, he proposed the theory that light was com-posed of waves vibrating in "a luminiferous ether", and that colours vibrated at different frequencies with different wave-lengths. In 1746, Swiss mathematician Leonard Euler came up with the mathematical form for this new wave theory.

One of the major consequences of these developments was the realization that the colours of the spectrum were not pro-duced in the medium, but at the boundaries of the medium – where the glass of the prism meets the surrounding air. In the same way, the colours of the rainbow emerge from sun-light at the edge of the rain droplets.

Rainbows

The colours of the rainbow have constantly delighted and puzzled mankind, a recurring challenge by the heavens to explain its charming celestial conundrum. Forming an arc across the rain-drenched skies, the rainbow was the mytho-logical bridge the Norsemen's fallen heroes took to reach the afterlife. To the Ancient Greeks, the rainbow was Iris, messenger of the gods.

Among those taking up the challenge – and perhaps the most appealing – was a 13th-century Dominican monk named Theodoric, who was born in Freibourg around 1250, but

The enchanting colours of the rainbow appear whenever sunlight is at a certain angle – 42 degrees – and the raindrops are the correct size – between 0.01 and 4 millimetres (0.0004 and 0.16 inches) in diameter (above and overleaf).

later studied in Paris. Like Newton after him, Theodoric was reticent in publishing his researches because his religious order did not encourage their devotees to pursue their own private pastimes.

Theodoric's independence of spirit had the additional effect of making him very critical of his own and others' claims. Perhaps for this reason his major work *De Iride* (On the Rainbow), completed by 1311, was remarkable because he attempted to support his every point by an empirical test, whether the point was derived from other sources or from his own. The two big questions he addressed were: first, how are the rainbow's colours formed, and second, why is the shape and order of the colours always the same?

Most previous commentators had thought the colours were really there, produced in an interaction between light from the Sun and the falling drops. Theodoric's explanation was very complex and completely wrong! He had no idea of the concept that light was a continuous spectrum of frequencies, but he believed there were four distinct radiant colours – red, yellow, green, and blue. Red, being clearest, appeared nearest to the surface, while blue and green were from the deepest parts of the water droplet. Theodoric did, however, uncover the idea that colours arise from differential refraction.

René Descartes took up the Rainbow Challenge, and his 1637 account is suspiciously similar to Theodoric's, whom he completely failed to acknowledge. Descartes did make one vital discovery: the maximum elevation of the bow is 42 degrees. Imagine you are watching a downpour of raindrops illuminated by parallel rays of bright sunlight. As each rain-drop (no bigger than four millimetres across) falls and makes an angle of 42 degrees with the observer, the white light of the Sun is refracted into colours by the drop – first red, then all the colours through to violet. The raindrops split white light into colours, and the rainbow shimmers into view.

Waves and electromagnetism

The English physicist Thomas Young finally proved that light behaved as a wave in 1803 in one of the most famous experiments in the history of physics. It changed the way scientists viewed the nature of light.

Young's experiment was simple: he shone a beam of light on to a sheet of paper through two parallel vertical slits, creating a pattern of alternate light and dark bands. He realized that these alternate bands could only be caused by interference between waves: where the peaks of waves overlapped they reinforced one another and became brighter; where they did not they cancelled each other out and created a dark band. Young was convinced he had found the solution to a major dilemma over the dual wave-particle nature of light.

The problem was defined by what happens to a light beam when it passes through an opening: if the opening is square, like a window, there is a clear sharp shadow of the window on the wall beyond. If, however, the opening is a narrow slit, the light does not cast a sharp slit-like image but spreads out like a fan. This is diffracted light.

Young's double-split experiment produced a result that was quite unpredicted. Shining the light beam on the two vertical slits should have intensified the diffracted light, but instead the image on the farther wall was a series of bands, with the brightest of them in the centre. Only when one of the slits was covered up did the diffracted light image appear.

Where did these waves come from and what were they made of? In 1864, Scottish physicist James Clerk Maxwell built on the work of Michael Faraday and others and developed the first unified field theory, which revealed the unifying laws governing electric and magnetic forces. He realized that light was one of many electromagnetic waves, part of a much bigger spectrum of energy. These waves had an electrical and a magnetic component vibrating at right angles to one another.

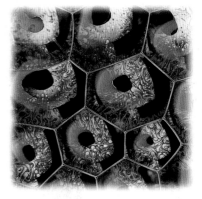

Thin films, such as those in a soap bubble (above) or the oil on the surface of water, break up white light into colours. The colour depends on the thinness of the film – for example, film as thin as a blue wavelength appears blue.

Particles, waves or both?

Light was born at the Big Bang – the start of all matter, space, energy and time. When new stars are born (above), a version of this explosion occurs, but on an extremely small scale.

When the solar wind sweeps through the Earth's ionosphere, glorious curtains of light can be witnessed in the high latitudes (opposite). In the northern hemisphere, these are known as the aurora borealis, or northern lights. In the south, they are termed the aurora australis, or southern lights.

At the beginning of the 20th century, the electromagnetic spectrum of energies was making headlines: X-rays, alpha, beta, and gamma radiation, and radio waves were all under investigation. The atom itself was no longer believed to be indivisible – it was known that it contained electrons as well as the promise of other subatomic particles. The stage was set for the return of the particle properties of light.

In 1900, the physicist Max Planck discovered one of the most useful facts about radiation: its energy was related to its frequency by a constant: 0.00000000000000000000000000006624, roughly. Until then, scientists had been puzzled by the photoelectric effect: the fact that when they shone pure violet light on to a metal plate, the plate emitted a shower of electrons. The number of electrons is dependent on the frequency of the light (lower frequencies produce fewer electrons), and not on its intensity as might be expected. Planck's constant gave scientists a measure of the energy, or quantum, of the radiation. For example, the quantum of red light is only half as energetic as the quantum of violet light.

The career of Albert Einstein was inextricably linked with his research into the nature of light. Einstein used this photoelectric effect to prove that light behaves as if it were made up of particles. Einstein supposed that all light is composed of individual discontinuous particles, or grains of energy, which he called photons. When these photons hit an electron, the result was like the collision of two billiard balls. The velocity with which electrons fly off the plate was proportional to the energy content of the arriving photons and this in turn depended on their frequency. This photoelectric effect is used in many ways today, including television – the picture on the screen is caused by the arrival of electrons, carefully controlled by magnetic fields so that they land in specific places.

Einstein's new idea of light containing photons was in conflict with Young's wave notion of light. The conflict remains

to this day: is light made of waves or particles – or both? We cannot answer this fully until we understand how electricity, magnetism, and gravitation work.

I myself find no difficulty with reconciling the two great controversies regarding light because I can envisage a wave composed of particles. For me, the electric field is a space filled with charged particles, and the density of the particles defines the strength of the field. So who was right about the nature of light?

In trying to explain the still extant paradox, scientists have come up with some ridiculous answers: Einstein, for example, speculated that photons were guided by "ghost waves". A non-starter, Einstein! In 1924, as quantum theory and "the new physics" unfolded, the Danish physicist Niels Bohr and two colleagues, H. A. Kramers and John Slater, suggested that the waves in question were "probability waves". These are mathematical entities by which physicists could predict the probability of certain events occurring or not.

Some creatures, many of which live in deep sea or areas where there is little natural light, produce their own living light. Lightbulb tunicates (*Clavelina lepadiformis*) glow in the waters of southwest England. Their light is produced by chemical reactions inside special light organs in the body.

Physicists had come up against something that Aristotle had pointed at: the concept of "potential", a tendency for some-thing. The 20th-century German scientist Werner Heisenberg described this as "something standing in the middle between the idea of an event and the actual event, a strange kind of physical reality just in the middle between possibility and reality". Gary Zukav, in his book *The Dancing Wu Li Masters* (1979) concluded that "Physicists found themselves dealing with energy that somehow processed information (which made it organic), and unaccountably presented itself in pat-terns (waves). In short, physicists found themselves dealing with Wu Li – patterns of organic energy."

Until now photons have been assumed to be composed of pure energy with no mass. But let us suppose that light is energy, with a material content that is very thinly spread. As the energy of light becomes more and more concentrated, so it slows down and condenses and becomes more and more like the materials we are familiar with in our world – our own bodies, for example.

So, ultimately, on this model, we may all be concentrations of energy. Just imagine the consequences of that: when I move my arm, it is the energy contained in the material of my arm that moves to a different place! In scientific language, all I am suggesting with this notion is to rearrange Einstein's famous equation $E = mc^2$ by saying that $m = E/c^2$. In other words, all mass (material) equals E (energy) divided by c^2 (the speed of light squared). All matter is simply concentrated energy. That was more or less what Wu Li was: patterns of organic energy. Wu can mean matter or energy, and Li means universal order or universal law.

In this world of the new physics, matter and energy are interchangeable: if matter sheds its mass and travels with the speed of light we call it radiation or energy. Conversely, if energy congeals and becomes inert and we can ascertain its mass, we call it matter.

Like Clerk Maxwell, I like to think of the universe as being connected in some way, perhaps because of being filled with electrons in fields of various densities. To the extent that electrons are all the same (the electrons in an atom of gold are indistinguishable from the electrons in an atom of lead), then there is a universal law or order already in place. Any change of any electron's position is relayed across the entire universe.

Why are electrons so useful to organic life? The first subatomic particles to be identified and the lightest, electrons are stable, interchangeable, and always carry a negative charge – which makes them good messengers. More importantly, electrons do not decay into other particles – hence their ubiquitous use in forming the bonds that bind molecules together.

Fractals (above) are patterns of self-organizing energy that repeat themselves *ad infinitum* according to established mathematical rules.

The Sun's cocktail of radiation

"Every kind of light has its beginnings in atoms" wrote the renowned writer and physicist, E. N. da C. Andrade. And most of the light in our environment reaches us from the atoms of the Sun. For this star of ours is an enormous nuclear reactor, a huge furnace of atoms and their subatomic particles – electrons, protons, neutrons, and so on.

Every single moment in time, countless millions of hydrogen atoms in the Sun are being transformed into helium atoms and, in the process, generating astonishingly huge amounts of energy. Matter is turned to energy at a rate of four million tonnes a second, creating a rich cocktail of electromagnetic radiation that spreads out in all directions.

In this cocktail there is just about every kind of electro-magnetic radiation – from X-rays through the spectrum to radio waves. Much is absorbed by Earth's atmosphere before it reaches us. What we do receive is infrared – which we feel as heat – visible light, and ultraviolet radiation.

As this electromagnetic energy radiates through space and time, it can be envisaged as behaving like vibrating waves that travel at the same very fast speed. The power and the quality of a particular energy resides in its wavelength and the frequency with which the wave vibrates. The family of infrared waves, for example, have longer wavelengths (from 1100 nanometres to 700 nanometres) than visible light (red begins at approximately 700 nanometres and violet ends at about 400 nanometres) and vibrate at lower frequencies. The ultra-violet waves are shorter still – from 400 nanometres to 290 nanometres – and vibrate at even higher frequencies.

Solar radiation reaching Earth does not contain equal amounts of these three families of radiation. For instance, there is a greater proportion of visible light than ultraviolet radiation; and of the visible light, there are more of the blue and green wavelengths than the reds and yellows.

The colours of light

Colour	Wavelength in nanometres
Red	700–625
Orange	625–595
Yellow	595–570
Green	570–495
Blue	495–440
Indigo	440–410
Violet	410–380

The white light emitted by the Sun is an incoherent mixture of all the different wavelengths in the visible spectrum. The image opposite shows white light made coherent by separating colours into radiating groups – from red, through yellow, green and blue, to violet (a mixture of red and blue).

Electrons and light

Forked lightning is a huge electrical spark, caused by the immense build-up of static electricity in thunderclouds. It is the perfect example of the remarkable speed of light – electromagnetic energy racing through the super-charged air in an instant.

Electrons give us the clue to why all electromagnetic waves, including light, travel at the same extremely fast speed. In fact, nothing travels faster than light – about 3×10^8 metres per second or approximately 300,000 kilometres per second in air. The waves are known to travel more slowly in water, but the principal interest of scientists was always to measure the speed of light through free space.

For multicellular creatures such as ourselves, however, it is the passage of electrons through the aqueous solutions of our body that count. These solutions are saline so the ions of positively charged sodium and negatively charged chlorine can assist in the conduction process: salty water carries electric currents far better than distilled water. It is only by the passage of electrons that the trillions of cells in a body can receive its co-ordinating instructions at lightning speed.

One example is the human heart: our heart muscles are controlled not by nervous conduction but by electric fields. Another is the brain, whose rhythms have defied functional explanation ever since their discovery. These rhythms can be picked up anywhere on the body, almost without any loss of signal strength, thanks to electrons.

The fact that light travels at a finite but very high speed was first discovered in 1676 by a Danish astronomer Ole Christian Roemer. He observed that the times at which the moons of Jupiter appeared to pass behind the planet were not evenly spaced, as one would expect if they went around it at a constant rate. Because his estimates of the distance between Jupiter and Earth were not accurate, his calculation of the speed of light was only 226,000 kilometres a second, but it was nevertheless not a bad first approximation.

It was not until much later that scientists began a proper assault on accurately describing the speed of light. James Clerk Maxwell, in his exposition of the electromagnetic theory of light, chronicled the various attempts to measure it. The French physicist H.L. Fizeau made the first of these in 1849. He set up an ingenious method of measuring the velocity of light in the laboratory which was consistent with Roemer's astronomical study.

Between 1856 and 1890, there were at least 15 studies that reported virtually the same answer. Maxwell himself went further, saying that light was an electromagnetic disturbance propagated in the same medium through which other electromagnetic actions are transmitted. He also explored the fact that a magnetic field has an effect on light, showing thereby that electrons were involved in light, though the electron itself had not yet been discovered or named at that time.

Clerk Maxwell had his suspicions about the existence of the electron, however. He wrote: "We are so little acquainted with the details of the molecular constitution of bodies that it is not probable that any satisfactory theory can be formed relating to a particular phenomenon, such as that of the magnetic action on light, until we learn something more definite about the properties which must be attributed to a molecule in order to satisfy the conditions of the observed facts."

He went on: "I think we have good evidence for the opinion that some phenomenon of rotation is going on in the magnetic field, that this rotation is performed by a great number of very small portions of matter, each rotating on its own axis, this axis being parallel to the direction of the magnetic force, and that the rotations of these different vortices are made to depend on one another by means of some kind of mechanism connecting them."

With this last sentence Clerk Maxwell had, in 1892, all but described the electron – it would be discovered by English physicist Sir Joseph John Thomson five years later – and had recognized the dependence of light on its connected nature.

The colour of every flower comes from the Sun, just as John Stewart Collis, poet, scientist, and scholar, says in *The Vision of Glory* (Penguin, 1975): "…that yellow on the daffodil, that red on the rose was eight minutes ago in the Sun."

Light penetrates the body

The poet William Blake once said that the universe could
sense the cry of a wounded hare. If such sensitivity is possible,
then a beam of light is an enormous input into any organic
body, since it represents trillions of electron movements. But
if the notion has currency, then the idea that light cannot
penetrate deep into the interior of a human being has to be
abandoned, too. Is there any evidence that the light falling on
the skin surface has an effect deep inside the body?

Several observations suggest this is exactly what happens.
Light does seem to have an effect on the suprachiasmatic
nuclei, where the two optic nerves cross in the middle of the
brain, although this may result from changes in the passage of
neuronal firings down the optic nerve, and not directly from
the incidence of light.

More important is the recent discovery that when light enters
the eye, some 20 percent of it carries on past the retina and
reaches vital components of the brain, especially the hypo-
thalamus, the pituitary gland, and of course the pineal gland
(see page 50). By this means, light (and by implication all
kinds of electromagnetic fields) can regulate the majority
of our life processes, including hormone production, stress
response, the autonomic nervous system, and the limbic system that is the seat of our emotions. Apart from these, the
light – once inside us – can affect our metabolism and even
our reproductive functions.

A medium for our eyes

Eyes probably developed from the amoeba onwards. If an
amoeba's surface had a small indentation in it, then light
would cause a shadow on the opposite side of the hollow.
If the light then moved, the shadow would also move, and
photosensitive chemicals – molecules that are sensitive to the
difference between light and dark – could serve as a warning
to the amoeba that a predator or prey might be near. From
such humble beginnings our "modern" eyes could have

developed, complete with the rod and cone cells which allow monochrome and colour vision respectively. Today the light falling on one eye is still decoded by the nerve cells in the opposite hemisphere in the brain – an echo of the amoeba.

Other creatures sense light directly through the skin. Worms, for example, have photoreceptors (cells that are sensitive to light) in the basal part of the skin's epidermis, especially at the front end, where there are distinctly lens-like structures. These receptors are photopositive to weak light and photonegative to strong light, and also seem (albeit crudely) to differentiate some frequencies.

We still have not tackled the puzzle of why organic life chose that particular part of the electromagnetic spectrum to sense the movement, form, and colour of other materials. One of the reasons may be that the higher the frequency the better the definition. In the 1930s, Royle Rife devised a microscope using not visible but ultraviolet light, which has a higher frequency than visible light. This enabled him to obtain much sharper pictures and much higher useable magnifications.

But the upper part of the UV spectrum is hazardous to our health, so this constituted a limit for sight sensing. Moreover, Rife began to discover that every microbe had a specific frequency to which it was sensitive and by applying the specific frequencies he could destroy it (a discovery which did not go down too well with the pharmaceuticals industry).

Another reason that evolution took the path it did might be to do with resonance. Visible light has an average 500 nanometre wavelength, say half a micron, and most of our cells have an extracellular matrix of about the same distance, stretching outwards from the cell membrane. Therefore, one could speculate that some of the glycoprotein strands in the membrane would be resonated by electromagnetic energy in the visible light bandwidth.

Natural daylight consists of all of these frequencies and more, including ultraviolet (UV). The spectacular effects when UV is introduced by hemo-irradiation into the blood stream or by fibre optics into tumours will be discussed later. Artificial light may not have all the components of daylight, however, and this, as will be seen, is important for health. Experiments conducted with standard fluorescent lighting have shown that it triggers stress-type levels of cortisol and ACTH (adreno-corticotrophic hormone) in the blood. From this work, some experts believe that the fluorescent lights used in schools may be responsible for the increase in hyperactivity seen today. In 1982, research carried out at the London School of Hygiene and Tropical Medicine in 1982 reported higher levels of cancer in fluorescent-lit offices.

The sensitivity of our eyes

But why should only the visible light frequencies have been chosen by Nature for our electromagnetic field and radiation sensors? When electrons are discharged in a vacuum they give out a green glow, which indicates that they are pulsing in the 500-nanometre wavelength. This gives us another clue why Nature should have chosen visible light frequencies to convey information centred on 500 nanometres – Nature had discovered the usefulness of the electron. The electron itself was discovered a century ago and its importance only about 80 years ago – an astonishing fact when we review the technological progress humans have made by its means since then.

The blue/purple cells in the retina of an eye (opposite) are the rods that are sensitive to dim light but not to colours. Light falling on the end of a rod triggers an electric impulse that travels along the optic nerve to a particular site in the visual cortex of the brain.

The fact that our eyes are capable of such extraordinary feats depends on the rod and cone cells in the retina (there are three types of cone cells and each type has different spectral responses). The rod cells incorporate discs of photosensitive membrane which are sequentially renewed every 15 minutes of our life, the newly formed discs gradually moving down the rod towards the pigmented epithelial cells at the back of the eye. Cones have these discs, too, but they are not constantly being replaced.

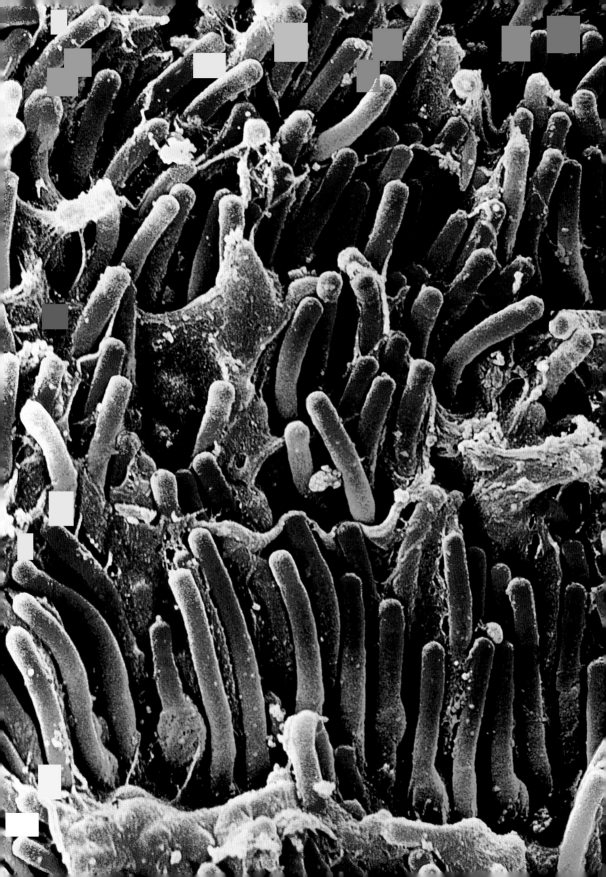

Individual photons are absorbed by a molecule that is known as rhodopsin embedded in the discs and, by a complicated amplification process, sodium ions are in turn prevented from entering the cell through their normal channels for about a second. This causes a massive electric charge to build up, enough to send a neural impulse to the occipital lobes. Thus the means of vision is based on the effect of electric charges.

The system must be even more subtle. By exposing rats to light sources of different colours (or wavelengths, because these are mutually determined), it has been demonstrated that certain colours are more effective in inhibiting the activity of the enzyme HIOMT, and thus melatonin production, than others. Green, for example, is more effective in inhibiting melatonin synthesis by the pineal, while red is completely ineffective: we have our own in-built photographic dark-room! Blue is fairly effective, yellow less so, while ultraviolet has a definite but weak inhibitory action.

Information transfer

There is a long history of the use of light for transmitting information. The 16th-century English astrologer John Dee invented what he called the "moonbeam telegraph", a system of relays placed 40 kilometres (25 miles) apart and consisting of towers with mirrors, whereby moonlight or sunlight could be reflected. It was successfully deployed between Gyor and Prague to relay to Emperor Rudolf II news of the recapture of the fortress of Gyor from the Turks by Hungarian commandos in the 17th century.

The eyes of all creatures, such as birds, reptiles, insects, and mammals, transform light into electrical impulses that travel to the brain and allow us to see the world around us. But sight is only part of the eye's function. Light enters the body primarily through the eyes and reaches the brain, where it has a profound influence on the body's processes.

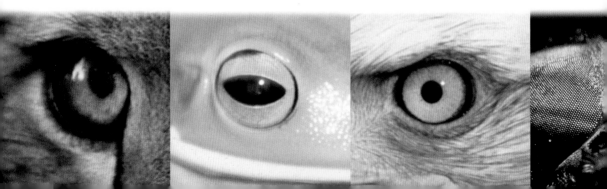

We now use radio waves at the speed of light to broadcast news and communications around the world, but as concerns over the possible adverse effects on our health of such waves grow, and the air waves leave no frequency unoccupied, so there is a concomitant growth in the use of fibre optics as a non-broadcast information transfer system. Indeed, light in fibre-optic cables can carry much more information than radio waves or telegraph wires.

To summarize, light is an electromagnetic wave of photons whose patterns can be seen not only in terms of their energy or frequency, which give rise to colour perception, but also as having a fundamental effect on many interior body processes. Furthermore, the possibility cannot be excluded that, as usual, Nature has anticipated our technology and also uses organic light to convey information around the trillions of cells in organic creatures. Later on, I explore the ways that this new molecular or quantum biology is being uncovered and the way the application of light can assist the healing process.

An object's colour is perceived by means of the frequency of visible light its surface reflects. A painter choosing his colours can judge with accuracy the precise shade of green, red or blue he requires. The ability of the eye to distinguish between frequencies is truly remarkable, and attracted the attention of one of the greatest 19th century physiologists, Hermann Helmholtz. He discovered that the eye was sensitive to a tiny amount of light energy – in quantum terms to as little as one single photon of light.

The power of sunlight

The warmth of sunlight on one's face is one of the basic pleasures of life – a pleasure that reaches to the very soul. When we feel light on our skin we instinctively know it is beneficial, because we ourselves are derived from that radiation. Without the Sun's rays no life can exist on Earth and the physical reunion with sunlight rejoices in that recognition.

Scientists have to concede the truth of this. Both the ancient Greeks and modern medicine confirm that sunlight is a potent bactericide. Cover an open wound from light and you risk infection. Sunlight metabolizes vitamin D, without which we are prone to calcium deficiency. It is the Sun that provides us with warmth, nourishes our crops, counts our days, and enriches our visual experience of life.

For this reason, we should try to make sure we spend at least half an hour a day outside, in natural light. The dangers of overexposure to the Sun's rays are well known, but had we not tampered with the delicate mantle of the ionosphere, the more damaging elements of solar energy could never have reached Earth they way they now do. Most of us now spend most of our time indoors, and our homes and offices should, ideally, be filled with natural light, not fluorescent tubes. Fluorescent light is suspected in more than one serious scientific study of increasing the likelihood of cancer.

With hospitals nowadays teeming with bacteria for which there is no antibiotic remedy, new methods need to be deployed, and those proving most effective beam the same sort of frequencies as those that come from the Sun at the infected area. A recent outbreak in Texas of the dreaded methycillin-resistant *Staphylococcus aureus* (MRSA) could only be brought under control by irradiation of the blood by UV light, a substitute for the Sun. It is high time we reminded ourselves of the Sun's healing powers.

Ultraviolet and heliotherapy

Though sunlight therapy has its roots in ancient history, the study of the healing effects of ultraviolet light only began in earnest in the 19th century in Scandinavia. It was a Danish professor, Niels Finsen, in the 1890s who first noticed that tubercular skin lesions were very common during the winter months but rare during summer.

Recognizing that this could be due to a lack of sunlight, he began treating lupus vulgaris (a tubercular skin condition) with carbon arc lamps, which radiate ultraviolet light. This was so successful that he set up a special clinic for sufferers and his innovations eventually gained him the Nobel Prize for being the first to succeed in treating skin tuberculosis. He also investigated the other end of the visible light spectrum and used red light in the treatment of smallpox lesions. Today Finsen is known as the father of photobiology.

Another 19th-century discovery was that the UV in sunlight could help the body make vitamin D. Made in response to sunlight, it is also called cholecalciferol, and is more effective than the synthesized version, ergocalciferol, used in vitamin tablets. Vitamin D is needed for the absorption of calcium and other minerals essential for the growth and maintenance of healthy bones and teeth. Deficiency can lead to rickets in the young and osteomalacia, or bone softness, in adults, both of which can be cured by sunlight but are exacerbated by lack of light. A study carried out at the Minerals Metabolism Unit at the Leeds General Infirmary in England, discovered many more instances of osteomalacia in postmortem examinations conducted in the winter than in summer.

Sunlight, Nature's bactericide

A further example of the beneficial effects of sunlight was discovered on a window-ledge of an Oxford College. In 1877 two English researchers, Arthur Downes and Thomas Blunt, performed an experiment in which they sterilized eight normal test tubes, filled them with Pasteur's solution (a sugar solution which encourages bacterial growth) and stopped the ends loosely with cotton wool. Four of the tubes were encased in lead to exclude all light and the other four were placed in the sunlight on a window-ledge for a month.

The lead-shielded tubes became "distinctly and uniformly milky" whereas the solution in the exposed tubes remained clear. This turbidity was found by microscopic examination to be due to swarms of bacteria. The effect was seen irrespective of the temperature, ruling out warmth as a factor, but did reflect whether the days were cloudy or not.

The authors reported to the Royal Society, "We find that the contents of a tube, which remain perfectly clear as long as they are freely exposed to the sun's rays, swarm with bacteria after being deprived of light". They also experimented with urine and hay infusion, finding that the urine from the lead-encased tube "was so offensive as to render the examination of even a drop a disagreeable task. It contained both rods and dumbbells in great numbers, and an abundance of the micro-cocci…". The implication was very clear: sunlight acted as a natural sterilizer.

Downes and Blunt did not realize that it was the UV component of sunlight that was responsible for the sterilization of bacteria, but they did start finding out that availability of oxygen was also a factor. It was a Swiss doctor, Auguste Rollier, who, early in the 20th century, narrowed down the beneficial effect to UV. His clinic in Leysin, a town high in the Swiss Alps, was devoted to curing tuberculosis with sunlight, and his book *La Cure du Soleil* sets out his reasoning for locating his clinic at 1,500 metres (5,000 feet): "because the air is transparent and easily traversed by the Sun's rays, which pass without absorption."

Rollier recognized the power of the Sun and took great care to expose his patients very gently at first, increasing their time

Children at the sanatorium run by Auguste Rollier in Leysin in the Swiss Alps took their lessons outdoors in order to get the benefit of the Sun's healing rays as they studied. Notice that all wear protective sunhats.

outdoors little by little each day. At first Rollier's theories were mocked, but 20 years later there were sunlight clinics in many parts of the world for the treatment of tuberculosis. Other diseases treated by heliotherapy included colitis, gout, anemia, cystitis, arteriosclerosis, rheumatoid arthritis, eczema, acne, asthma and burns. Another early discovery was that ultraviolet radiation from the Sun can lower a patient's blood pressure. The effect of even one exposure can last as long as five or six days.

But in the late 1930s, when light therapies were at the height of their success, penicillin, the first antibiotic, was becoming available. Medics and patients alike embraced the new pharmaceutical cures and sunlight therapy was forgotten.

Healing powers

Now, at the beginning of the 21st century, people are once again coming to realize the healing benefits of sunlight. For example, another condition linked to vitamin D deficiency and more common than osteomalacia is osteoporosis, which affects one in three women over 50 and one in 12 men. In this disorder, the bone starts to lose its mass, becomes fragile and may eventually collapse. The best way to avoid osteoporosis is to get plenty of vitamin D and calcium during childhood and adolescence and to take some weight-bearing exercise throughout adult life. It is also important to continue to get adequate exposure to sunlight in old age. Taking a stroll in the local park and sitting for a while in the sunlight on a park bench is an ideal way for elderly people to make sure they receive their daily quota of vitamin D.

Calcium has functions in delivering important information to cells as well as providing the hardness in our bony skeletons. Few people realize that light (as well as other electromagnetic frequencies in the extremely-low-frequency, or ELF, range) is an essential component if we are to absorb calcium into our bones and thereby strengthen them. ELF electromagnetic

Sun-therapy clinics, such as those run by Auguste Rollier for the treatment of tuberculosis, were always located at high altitudes (opposite). The combination of the cool, pure air and the Sun's rays maximized healing benefits.

fields have been used to treat fractures that do not heal normally by means of a technique pioneered at Columbia University, New York, which involves passing a pulsed field through the limb. And in a study of elderly men in a rest home at Boston, Massachusetts, the improved absorption of calcium with the aid of natural sunlight was demonstrated. A number of volunteers were isolated from natural light and exposed only to artificial light of various kinds. After seven weeks of this isolation, the men were able to absorb only 40 percent of the calcium contained in their food. Those who continued with the isolation for another month absorbed 25 percent less than before.

The same effect was seen in an experiment carried out on young men: after two months of isolation from natural light they lost 50 percent of their vitamin D levels and began to lose more calcium than they were ingesting, suggesting that their bones were beginning to give up their calcium. The practical moral of this study is clear: get outside and reap the benefits of sunlight, whatever your age.

In considering the benefits of natural light, one must bear in mind that in today's office-bound and indoor society we are prone to pack all our sunlight exposure into an annual summer vacation. This dramatic form of exposure to the sun is not beneficial and can be positively harmful. It is much more helpful to get a little sunlight gradually day by day, since over-exposure of the unconditioned bare, pale skin is damaging and may even be carcinogenic.

Ultraviolet: the promise and the perils

Today we hear much about the perils of sunlight while its beneficial aspects are played down. The concerns of the National Radiological Protection Board (NRPB) and other regulatory bodies about elective exposure to sunlight result from the changes in the ionosphere, which allow more of the harmful end of the UV spectrum to reach the Earth.

The NRPB has recently published a document on elective exposure to solar ultraviolet radiation. This has become an important issue because of quite proper public concerns about continued depletion of the ozone layer, blamed on an accumulation of chlorofluorocarbons (CFCs). Though CFC production has been curtailed, the ozone layer continues to be depleted: one theory is that radio waves broadcast from Earth are eroding the ozone layer from below. Radio waves are bounced off the ionosphere's layers in order to get around the curvature of the Earth. That is why the so-called "holes" are appearing above reflective white surfaces such as the ice caps and Switzerland, and above cities such as New York and London, which have large electromagnetic traffic.

Belated attempts are being made to increase the amount of info-traffic via fibre optics stretched along the nation's power-lines, so reducing electromagnetic pollution. But the problems will probably continue until city dwellers in the northern hemisphere start to suffer the same incidence of conditions such as skin cancer and cataracts as those in Australia and South America. Only then will they understand the dangers.

Ten benefits of sunlight

In his book *Light: Medicine of the Future,* light therapist Dr Jacob Liberman lists ten important benefits of sunlight:

1   Allows the production of vitamin D in the body
2   Lowers blood pressure
3   Increases the efficiency of the heart in pumping blood
4   Improves electrocardiogram readings
5   Reduces levels of cholesterol and hypertension
6   Assists weight loss
7   Is an effective treatment of psoriasis
8   Increases levels of sex hormones
9   Helps alleviate asthma and other lung disorders
10 Increases production of solitrol, a hormone that affects mood

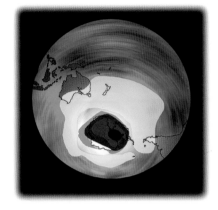

The ozone layer, which is between the trophosphere and the stratosphere, normally contains high concentrations of ozone gas. Ozone absorbs much of the Sun's ultraviolet radiation before it reaches Earth. The red and purple area over Antarctica (above) indicates not a "hole" but a significant thinning of ozone concentration.

In every Italian town there is a piazza – an ideal spot to enjoy the late afternoon sunshine and a talk with old friends (overleaf).

Safe sun

An Australian sun awareness campaign, known as "slip, slop, slap", aims to encourage children to protect themselves from sunburn. The advice is to "slip" on a shirt for protection, "slop" on some some sunscreen, and "slap" on a hat.

Taken sensibly, sunlight is good for us. As we have learned, the Sun's rays have many benefits – they have a healing effect, they synthesize vitamin D in the body, and they boost the immune system. But too much sunshine – sunburn – is clearly harmful and needs to be avoided. Sunburn ages the skin and can even lead to skin cancer, the second most common cancer in the USA and UK. Recent studies indicate that one in five people will develop some form of melanoma. The number of new cases of skin cancer increases every year and incidence doubled in the 20 years leading up to 2000.

The cause of skin cancer is nearly always overexposure to certain kinds of ultraviolet radiation, from the Sun or from a sunbed. Ultraviolet is also reflected off light-coloured surfaces, especially water, sand, and snow, and this increases its strength and the likelihood of sunburn. You can get burnt through shallow water or light cloud: up to 75 percent of the Sun's rays can still reach you.

The skin darkens during tanning because it is damaged: the colour, the skin's attempt to protect itself, is a response to the UVB rays, producing a pigment called melanin. It is UVB that leads to cancer-causing cells, while UVA can penetrate deep into the tissues, causing premature ageing and increasing the cancer-causing potential of UVB. Be aware of your skin, and if you have a mole that is changing size, shape, or colour, or that is itching or bleeding, see your doctor. Skin cancers can be cured if treated early.

So who is most at risk from skin cancer? In a study carried out in the 1980s, researchers found that, contrary to previous belief, those most at risk were people who spent most of their working life indoors, not those who worked mainly out of doors. People with the lowest risk were those who regularly spent time in the sun. This experiment bears out the current view that the worst way of exposing yourself to sunlight is for prolonged concentrated periods – the traditional summer vacation on the beach. Instead, go out into the sun regularly for short periods. Do this all year round, whatever the weather, not just in high summer and you will reap the advantages of natural light to the full.

So how do you get the benefits of the sunlight without the dangers? Here is some advice:

• Spend at least 30 minutes a day out of doors, taking a walk, working in the garden or just sitting. Even being in the shade is beneficial. If you want to stay outside for an hour or more that is fine, but build up to this gradually. Don't suddenly sit out at midday in high summer. When indoors, sitting by an open window can ensure that you receive the full spectrum of sunlight.

• Do not allow your skin to burn. Sunburn shows that the skin has been damaged. Aim instead for a slow, gentle tan to build up the skin's own protection.

• Early morning sunlight in the cooler air is more beneficial than baking at midday. Exposure to direct sunlight at over 25°C (77°F) should be avoided if possible.

• If you travel to a hotter climate than you are used to, stay out of the sun for a few days while you acclimatize.

• Wear a hat to protect your head and neck.

• As John Ott (see pages 104–5) discovered, glasses, sunglasses and contact lenses filter out UV rays and reduce the benefits of healthy sunbathing. Unless the day is very bright, sunbathe without glasses of any kind.

• Don't cram all your sunbathing into one summer fortnight. Take it gently from spring onwards.

• Have a healthy diet. Research suggests that eating plenty of fruit and vegetables, rich in antioxidants, can help minimize sun damage and protect the skin from damage by UV rays.

• Don't put too much reliance on sunscreens. Some research suggests that sunscreens can increase the risk of melanoma because they encourage people to spend longer in the sun. Sunscreens also inhibit vitamin D production in the skin.

Skin types

Obviously the amount of sunlight you can take with safety
depends to a large degree on your skin type. Those with paler
skins are at much greater risk of burning and sun damage
than those with darker skins. There are four main skin types
and each reacts in a different way to the sun.

• Fair: white skin, freckles, blue eyes, red or blond hair. This
group burn very easily and do not tan. They need very careful exposure, preferably on cooler days, in order to build up
tolerance to the sun without burning.

• Medium light: fair skin, blond or brown hair. This group
will tan in time but burn if proper care is not taken to build-
up sun exposure gradually.

• Medium dark: olive or light brown skin, dark hair and eyes,
such as people from China, Japan, Southeast Asia and the
Mediterranean countries. This group of people tans easily
but can also burn, particularly if they normally spend little
time in the sun.

• Dark: brown to black skin, dark hair and eyes. This group is
in little risk of burning, even after long periods in the sun.

Sun care for children

Never expose babies under the age of six months to direct
sunlight. Infants between six months and one year can be
exposed for short periods with a good sun hat and protective
clothing but not between 11 am and 2 pm in summer. Take
particular care on the beach, where the pale-coloured sand
reflects radiation upwards so that it reaches the face indirectly.
Use sun protection cream factor 25 or more.

Children can be gradually acclimatized to sunshine in the
place where they live, but take extra care when you go away
on vacation, particularly to a hotter country or area. The seaside is a pleasant but perilous place, not only because of the
stronger sunshine! Sea breezes can deceive you about the
strength of the Sun's rays, too, and you will only notice it
when the sunburn sets in in the evening.

The best advice is to dress children to minimize exposure
during the midday period, help them acclimatize to sunshine
in the earlier and less sunny parts of the year, and, when they
are old enough, explain the hazards of skin cancer from
excess exposure to the sun. As for adults, little and often is
the best strategem for sunbathing, whether it be on summer
vacation or at home.

Spending time outdoors, like these
people on Venice Beach, California,
is good for your health – as long as
you take proper care and avoid
sudden, long exposure to hot sun.

Full-spectrum light and SAD

Full-spectrum lighting is a light source that replicates as nearly as possible the spectral curve produced by the Sun. Numerous experiments have proved that full-spectrum lights can improve health and performance and decrease conditions such as headaches, depression, and fatigue. As people spend more time indoors, the implications of full-spectrum lighting become increasingly important.

Dr John Ott, a former time-lapse photographer at the Walt Disney studios, discovered some of the amazing properties of full-spectrum lighting when trying to film the flowering of a pumpkin. When he tried to grow pumpkins indoors under fluorescent light he found that the male flowers were healthy, but the female flowers died soon after they formed. When he used cool white light the reverse happened – the female pollen thrived but the male flowers died. Only full-spectrum, natural light was effective in developing full fertilization in the pumpkins.

Ott's film *Exploring the Spectrum* showed the effect of full-spectrum light on organisms. It demonstrated how in natural light the chloroplasts in plant cells move around in an orderly fashion. But in cells exposed to light with no UV component the chloroplasts' normal patterns were disturbed, and they tended to gather in one part of the cell. Red and blue filtered light also had a disruptive effect.

His interest aroused, Ott experimented with the effects of different sorts of light on animals. Mice kept in laboratory conditions under pink fluorescent light lived only 7.5 months on average and those under white light for an average 8.2 months, while those mice kept in natural daylight lived for 16.1 months on average and were in much better health.

As a result of his work, Ott coined the term malillumination. Malillumination means that the light to which the subject is exposed is not full spectrum but lacks some frequencies.

Imagine that white light is a balanced composite of the hues between infrared and ultraviolet. Shining light through a prism separates these out, revealing the range as a rainbow-like beam of coloured lights. It would appear that evolution has made use of all these in organic life, and taking any one of them away deprives the organism of ingredients essential for health. In experiments on caged rabbits Ott found that filtering out normal sunlight by using tinted glass to enclose their cages caused abnormal cell function in the pigment epithelial cells of the animals' retinas. These experiments confirmed that using the wrong kind of light (light from which some frequencies are missing) can actually damage plants and animals, and it raises questions about the effect on humans, too. People who habitually wear sunglasses or other tinted lenses could be affecting their personality if not also their well-being.

This passenger is wearing a "Jet Lag Visor", believed to lessen the symptoms of jet lag, during her flight. By shining bright light on the eyes, the visor aims to reset the body's biological clock, so synchronizing sleep/wake cycles with those at the passenger's destination.

Fluorescent light in schools

In a study of the effects of fluorescent lighting, pupils in two Florida classrooms were monitored using Ott's time-lapse photography techniques. This uncovered the clear evidence that fluorescent lighting leads to hyperactivity, irritability, and fatigue as well as attention deficits. Ott was instrumental in advising Duro-Test Corporation to add a phosphor to its fluorescent tubes so that they more nearly mimicked natural lighting, and thereby inspired the first full-spectrum lighting tube, called the VitaLite. VitaLite tubes are now in use in many countries, and users report better health, including a lowered incidence of headaches and absence of eye strain. Fluorescent tubes have also been under suspicion as causing increased skin cancers. My advice is to avoid them, except for the full-spectrum types.

Gradually, other scientists have followed Ott's lead in research on the use of light for plant and animal health and extended it to human beings. NASA, for example, now installs full-spectrum lighting in space craft.

Another researcher, Dr Fritz Hollwich confirmed John Ott's findings in a 1980 study reporting higher levels of the stress hormones ACTH and cortisol in subjects exposed to cool-white (non full-spectrum) lighting. These problems were totally absent when full-spectrum lighting was used. Cool-white tubes are deficient in the red and the blue-violet ends of the visible spectrum and these are necessary for health.

One thing to beware of with full-spectrum lighting is that some tubes do not maintain their full spectrum indefinitely, but can deteriorate with time. This means you should try to change the tubes every year if possible. Unfortunately, there is no inexpensive light meter that can tell you if the lamp is changing, only your own mood level, but forewarned is fore-armed. Another thing to watch is that the electronic ballast should be flicker free, and a low-frequency ballast may need changing for a higher frequency. Your electrical store should be able to supply this.

Seasonal defective disorder

Seasonal illness, and associated depression, has been known about for more than 2000 years, but it was only relatively recently given its modern name of SAD, or Seasonal Affective Disorder. Dr Norman E. Rosenthal is credited with having discovered the condition in 1981 and coining the term Seasonal Affective Disorder for the depression brought about by lack of daylight hours in winter (see pages 60–61). Nearly everyone experiences some change of mood and perhaps diminished energy in winter, but for some the effects are much more serious and lead to this debilitating illness.

It is thought that the condition is affected by the amount of light entering the eyes. In the darkness of night, the body produces a hormone called melatonin (see pages 50–57). In the morning, the bright light triggers melatonin production to stop and stimulates wakefulness. The theory is that in the dull days of winter some people find that not enough light is

A night-shift worker sits at his computer in a room with a simulated sunrise (opposite). In this experiment, electrodes attached to his head measure his brainwaves and facial responses. These show that the bright light of the "sunrise" increases his alertness and improves his performance in computerized logical reasoning tests.

received to trigger the waking-up process, which results in drowsiness and depression. Replacing the missing light by administering the correct amount of bright light early every day seems to alleviate the problem.

The symptoms of SAD affect four times as many women as men. They recur regularly each year in the early or late autumn and continue until spring. A diagnosis can be made if a person has suffered from typical symptoms for two or more consecutive winters, and other possible causes have been excluded. The SAD Association can supply medical information for doctors as well as patients (see page 151) for further details).

SAD symptoms differ from those of clinical depression in a number of ways. For example, SAD can cause carbohydrate craving, overeating, and weight gain, as opposed to weight loss and diminished appetite. Sufferers tend towards over-sleeping (hypersomnia) rather than insomnia, though they may also experience disturbed sleep with early morning waking. Other symptoms include low self-esteem, negative thoughts and feelings, apathy, despair, fatigue, concentration and memory difficulties, irritability, anxiety, tension, loss of libido, and gradual or sudden mood changes in spring.

Recognizing the need to simulate sunlight to treat SAD, a number of firms have developed special light boxes which have full-spectrum lighting and a brightness of at least 2500 lux – a lux is a unit of light intensity equivalent to light of one candle at a distance of 1.5 metres (5 feet). The boxes produce high light levels without ultraviolet and use the latest flicker-free high-frequency circuits. To give you an idea of relative light levels, a bright sunny day has a light level of around 100,000 lux. Though melatonin levels can change in response to levels of exposure as low as 200 lux for an hour, indoor lighting normally means illumination of the order of only 600 to 700 lux.

The newest light boxes provide light levels of about 10,000 lux and are highly effective for curing jet lag, premenstrual syndrome (PMS), and helping people with problems caused by shift work as well as seasonal affective disorder (SAD). Users sit in front of the light source for between 15 and 45 minutes each day.

It is important to take light therapy in the early morning if the aim is to cure SAD, since this induces a circadian phase shift. The bright light from the box causes the pineal gland to stop producing the nocturnal melatonin and triggers the waking-up process.

Light boxes for treating SAD should not be confused with the sunbeds in common use to obtain a tan. Sunbeds radiate large quantities of UV, whereas light boxes do not. You will not receive any UV from your light box, or full-spectrum light from your sunbed.

Treatment with bright light from a light box is effective in up to 85 percent of cases of medically diagnosed SAD. Sufferers from PMS may also benefit. It has no effect on non-SAD sufferers, so consult your GP or physician if in doubt about your condition. The following advice follows the guidelines given by the SAD Association.

A SAD sufferer sits in comfort watching television, while receiving her daily dose of bright light from her portable light box (above). This treatment has been proved to relieve symptoms in the majority of SAD patients.

Using a light box

When choosing a light box, the strength of light is of vital importance. You need at least 2500 lux for effective treatment of SAD symptoms. Most provide 10,000 lux, but this is only effective at close range. Broadly speaking, if you sit within 1 metre (3 feet) from a 10,000 lux unit you will receive at least 5000 lux. Light box suppliers can give information on the strength and range of different models. If time is at a premium or your symptoms are severe, choose a model that delivers the highest-strength light so that you need to spend less time sitting in front of it.

Natural daylight and bright white light tubes are available in light boxes and both are believed to be effective and safe. Your choice depends on personal preference. If you are not sure about the effectiveness of light boxes for your particular condition, some companies will hire out their equipment for a trial period (see page 151).

Place the box at an appropriate height so that it is directed at your eyes. Allow the lights to warm up, then start timing your session. Sit or stand at the manufacturer's specified distance from the box, and carry on with your everyday activities. You do not have to stare at the box, but you must keep your eyes open. Do not wear goggles or tinted lenses and follow the manufacturer's instructions carefully regarding timing and distance. Start using the box in early autumn, ideally before your symptoms appear, and increase the length of the sessions as winter advances. In time, you will be able to judge your daily dose of light therapy for yourself.

Morning light sessions are most beneficial for the majority of SAD sufferers. Try fitting a time-switch to your light box, and use it on waking. If you go out early, make time for at least a half-hour session before leaving, and finish your treatment later. But avoid using your light box in the evening, since this may cause sleep disturbances.

In general, aim to use your light box every day until spring, with an occasional day or two off. SAD symptoms will recur after three to four days without treatment. If you experience infrequent problems such as sore eyes or a slight headache (sometimes caused by staring at the light box), switch off the light box for a while and go back to it later. A few people have sleep problems or feel agitated when they first start light treatment. This may be a sign that they need to cut the length of their session or reschedule it to a different time. Finally, replace the light bulbs or tubes regularly, according to the manufacturer's advice.

Light and colour

The colours that we see affect our moods, and our moods determine our achievements and our actions. For example, American prisons have experimented, with some success, with pink-painted prison cells for violent inmates. The colour is believed to have a pacifying effect. The fact that colour can affect feelings and atmosphere is, of course, well recognized: we talk of "the blues" when we are feeling depressed. We call someone "yellow" when he or she is cowardly, and another "green" when he is a novice. We "see red", and "wave a red rag at a bull" to anger him. We give "black looks" to people.

It is as if we all have an inner spectrum of colours related to our moods, and by using these same colours externally we can influence our inner moods. This notion has been taken further by colour therapists and has a firm scientific basis.

Different colours seem to have important biological effects. In 1968 the biologists Oishi and Kato, from Kyoto University in Japan, painted the heads of Japanese quails with pigments that irradiated some with orange light and others with green light. They found that those exposed to orange light showed gonadal development, whereas those seeing only green did not. The same effect of orange-red light on gonadal development was reported by Dr J. Benoit in experiments on eyeless young ducks in which light was shone directly into the brain. The scientists proposed that the pineal gland (see page 50), too, may have a role in reproductive function, as well as its other duties, and melatonin has long been connected with influencing sexual activity: ovulation in females occurs when melatonin is at its lowest levels.

Not only animals but plants respond differently to different coloured lights. In the 19th century, General A. J. Pleasanton of Philadelphia claimed that grapevines grown in a greenhouse specially made with panes of blue glass as well as clear had a greatly increased yield. He found that they became very productive in the first and second year of growth, whereas normally the plants take at least six years to reach that stage of maturity. In 1895, another scientist in this field of research, C. Flammarion, claimed the reverse – that plants flourished best under red light. Others have since joined the debate with their own theories.

The experiments of acknowledged colour therapy expert Theo Gimbel, for example, showed that plants grown under red light were stunted, with small foliage. Green light produced brittle weak plants, but blue light gave well-developed plants with good foliage. Other colours in the visible range are found to have distinct physiological therapeutic effects on humans. Orange, for example, is traditionally the colour of stimulation, and green the colour of repose. Gimbel, who runs the Hygeia College of Colour Therapy in England, was born in Bavaria in 1921 and settled in Britain after World War II. His experiences in solitary confinement during the war, often in the dark, were the inspiration for forming the colour therapy practice that has made him famous all over the world.

The background to colour therapy

It is important to obtain corroborative and sound scientific evidence when claiming specific colour-healing bio-effects. Though little modern research has been done to date, the 19th century work is interesting. In 1877 Dr. Seth Pancoast published a book titled *Blue and Red Lights,* detailing his work on filtering sunlight through red or blue glass to treat the nervous system. Then, in 1878, Edwin Babbit's book *The Principles of Light and Colour,* on his work with coloured light, became a best seller. He used natural and artificial light with coloured filters and developed ways of focusing the light on the area of the body needing treatment. His devices almost certainly contained an element of UV. Babbit is also recorded as using solarized water – water which has been exposed to sunlight through a coloured filter of choice, and then given to the patient to drink.

The work of colour therapists has shown that wall colour, at home and in public buildings, affects the mood and well-being of the room's inhabitants. A warm orange (opposite), for example, has been shown to be stimulating, encouraging a joyful atmosphere.

Surpassing all these earlier therapists is Dinshah P. Ghadiali, who in 1934 published the three-volume *Spectro-Chrome Metry Encyclopaedia*. This work is effectively a home study course for Dinshah's theories. He combined the sciences of astronomy, physiology and radiology to argue that all their laws were ultimately an expression of vibrational frequency.

Dinshah (as he was called), being a physicist by training, recognized that every chemical element in an excited state emits a characteristic and distinctive set of coloured bands, called spectral emission lines, which are visible in a spectroscope. These are known as Fraunhofer lines. Moreover, when the excited element is exposed to white light it absorbs all the specific frequencies it had been emitting.

Considering the human being as a similar set of elements, Dinshah realized that the human body would absorb and emit specific light frequencies in the same way. From this beginning he devised a specific set of twelve coloured filters to match those of the body and used these to achieve spectacular healing results. The colours selected were red, orange, yellow, lemon, green, turquoise, blue, indigo, violet, purple, magenta, and scarlet. The filtered light was shone, or in Dinshah's words "tonated", from a projector onto the relevant part of the body to cure a variety of ailments. After years of practice, he identified a few fundamental patterns to help therapists determine which colours to use. For example, he found that purple, scarlet, and magenta were indicated in treatments relating to the heart and reproductive systems. Indigo was valuable in treating pain, injury, and bleeding.

Dinshah began his work in 1920. By 1926 even establishment clinicians were confirming the efficacy of the Dinshah filters, and Dinshah himself had gained four honorary medical degrees. A senior surgeon at a Philadelphia hospital lent her support to Dinshah's work, claiming "I can produce quicker and more accurate results with colours that with any or all other methods combined." Colour therapy was reported as having benefits for sprains, bruises, and trauma of all sorts, septic conditions, cardiac lesions, asthma, hay fever, corneal ulcers, inflammation of the eyes, glaucoma, and cataracts.

Dinshah also stated that human disease was evident in the aura around the body. He invented a home kit, called the Aluminium Spectro Chrome, so that anyone could shine his filters on their ailing body, using an automatic time-switch.

But eventually Dinshah's methods fell foul of orthodoxy. Dogged for years by the equivalent of today's US Food and Drug Administration (FDA), Dinshah, who practised in Philadelphia, was finally prohibited from using his techniques. Today it is still technically illegal in the USA to tell people about colour therapy.

Colour in classrooms

So far, we have confined the application of colour therapy to using specific machines. But of course our domestic environments permit us to colour the walls of our homes and offices, too. Dr Harry Wohlfarth and his associate Catherine Sam investigated the effects of full-spectrum lighting combined with particular warm wall colours in a school for handicapped children in Edmonton, Alberta. Their theories were based on ideas of Freud, who noted that one effect of trauma was a closed-down visual field, and those of H. Ertel, a German researcher, who found that the use of bright warm colours such as yellow and orange improved the intelligence quotient and academic achievement of schoolchildren.

A classroom in the Edmonton school was decorated in warm colours and full-spectrum lighting was installed. The children's behaviour and physical condition was monitored before and after the experiment. Their mean systolic blood pressure dropped 20 points after using the room for a period and there was a dramatic improvement in behaviour. But when the full-spectrum lighting was removed and ordinary fluorescent light replaced, their behaviour became disorderly once more and blood pressure increased. Astonishingly, the same results were recorded in blind as in sighted children.

The tests were replicated over a complete school year with four other Canadian schools: the control school had no full-spectrum lighting and no colour treatment, and it performed worst. The best performer was where both full-spectrum lighting and colour treatment had been applied.

Hyperactivity in young children is an increasing burden on parents today. One cause of this is the high field strength of ELF electric fields, given off by televisions, stereos, computers and other equipment, measured in the bedrooms of the sufferers. Barbara Meister Vitale, a well-known expert in this field, recommends placing pieces of coloured felt in the child's immediate environment to reduce hyperactivity and increase attention span. Her experiments showed red to be the most effective colour.

A different approach recommends the wearing of special tinted glasses. In 1988, on the US television programme *Sixty Minutes*, Helen Irlen, a psychologist from California, showed how non-reading, learning-disabled children were made into fluent readers by modifying the colours of light entering their eyes. Irlen's tinted spectacles need to be chosen by trial and error from a range of 140 tints. Much research remains to be done, but results so far have been encouraging.

Colours link indirectly to my laboratory's "hard" scientific approach to the endogenous fields of organic life. We have discovered that they have an important effect on lymphocyte competence, hence on health and well-being. Colours, in the form of electromagnetic energy of a specific frequency in the visible light range, directly affect the endogenous fields of the body. This is because any electric field will add to any other and thereby perturb it. Thus the electric component of any colour radiation will have a specific effect on the endogenous electric field of any living creature.

At present there does not exist any single instrument capable of simultaneously analysing the complex endogenous fields of the brain, where perhaps some 30,000 inter-hemispheral strands are at any one time creating electric fields for onward transmission through the body. Imposing colours on these has a clear physical effect, but more than that, the subtle energetic effects of colour can directly influence diseases.

Therapists such as Dr Richard Gerber claim that there is a connection between certain colours and the chakras – the metaphysical energy centres of the body. The suggestion is that the chakras, can be balanced and healed by the use of appropriate colours (see the chart below). As a biologist, I feel initially uncomfortable with this idea because scientists like to measure and define everything. I would like to see scientific studies confirming these theories. Surprisingly, a number of establishment scientists have begun along that path.

Colour	Chakra	Energies	Diseases affected
Violet	Crown	Higher mind	Mental disorders
Indigo	Pineal	Vision	Eye diseases
Blue	Throat	Self-expression	Thyroid, larynx
Green	Heart	Inner harmony	Heart, hypertension
Yellow	Solar plexus	Intellectual	Stomach, liver
Orange	Spleen	Assimilation	Lungs, kidneys
Red	Root	Vitality, creativity	Blood disorders

Colour therapists believe that each of the body's chakras, or energy centres, is linked to a particular colour (left). Illness or imbalance is treated by absorbing the appropriate colour physically, through the eyes and skin, and mentally, via meditation and visualization techniques.

Bring light into your home

"Glory be to God for dappled things. For skies of couple-colour as a brinded cow…" wrote the poet Gerard Manley Hopkins, mirroring our fascination with light and shade, tone and hue, colour and contrast. As author and environmentally aware architect David Pearson makes clear in his classic *New Natural House Book*, natural light is infinitely variable. It can range from the subtle, diffused light of a mist-filled morning to the dappled pattern of sunlight on leaves. For the good of your health and spirit, try to fill your home with as much natural light as possible.

Your house or apartment may only have windows at the front and back, but if you are building an extension you could add windows with other aspects. Bay windows, skylights, and clerestory windows (like the high-up narrow windows of some churches) add light and a sense of space to an existing room. So, too, does cross-lighting from windows on opposite sides. If you are adding windows, try to make sure that they have a purpose, such as bringing morning sun into a kitchen, or evening light into a sitting room.

Tall windows sweeping up to the ceiling can make a room seem vast and airy, but these need to be balanced with temperature considerations – large windows are colder. Adding a balcony to a narrow room can double the space, and plants will enjoy it too. Glasshouses or conservatories are another option. These have been used since Roman times, and are a wonderful way of creating a plant-filled indoor/outdoor haven, perfect for relaxing. With modern design features incorporated, they can look and feel stunning – particularly if you fill them with sweet-scented plants.

Lower floors which have little natural light can benefit from a device called a light tube – a tiny tubular skylight with a reflective shaft – that pipes in the daylight to dark spaces (see page 152). This is not hard to install and can dramatically increase the amount of light in a gloomy part of the house.

Huge skylights in the high roof make this studio into a dramatic, light-filled space (opposite). Research shows that living in low light levels results in an increase in depression and lethargy – a reason to make your home and work space as sunny and light as possible.

Make the most of sunlight

A shaft of golden light from a skylight (above) enlivens this dark, narrow staircase. Light used in this way becomes almost sculptural in the patterns it creates.

If you have a choice in the way you allocate you rooms in your home, try to make sure that you make the most of available sunlight. Bedrooms, for example, should face the rising Sun. Breakfast rooms should face the early sunlight, too, while kitchens, living rooms, and playrooms benefit most from the late morning, afternoon, and early evening sunshine.

If you work from home, your workspace needs natural light during the middle of the day. A study that is mostly used in the evening can be located on the north side of the house, which is darker. Storage spaces and garages are better on the cooler, darker side of the house, and if added on to an existing building, they can provide additional insulation.

David Pearson has the following suggestions for making the most of the available sunlight:

• As far as possible, increase the amount of daylight coming in from the outside. Use a light-coloured paving under windows to reflect plenty of light into the room. Apply light paint to garden walls or to outside walls next to windows. Install a pond and keep any overhanging trees and shrubs well pruned so that they don't obstruct too much light.

• Increase the amount of reflected daylight from surfaces inside the room. Use light-coloured furnishings and carpets and hang mirrors.

• Allow light to flood into a room by keeping the glass clean and clearing away obstructions from windows. Use curtain fixtures that allow you to draw the curtains right back to clear the window area.

• In order to maximize winter sunlight, yet have some shade from glaring summer sun, grow deciduous trees, climbing plants and bushes near windows on the sunny side of your house or building.

If you cannot manage any structural alterations, concentrate on interior decor to make your home seem lighter and brighter. Painting walls "off-white" (as opposed to brilliant white, which may feel cold and clinical) will help. So will laying pale wooden flooring, and giving dark, unattractive furniture a lick of limewash, or covering it with a light-coloured "throw".

Mirrors can make an amazing difference to the light in a room. Place them on window reveals (the vertical side-walls of a window at an angle to the adjoining wall) or on walls opposite the windows, and see how they completely alter the mood and tone. In Scandinavian countries, where winter light is at a premium, the interior decor bears witness to this. Tiny mosaic mirror tiles create movement and sparkling patterns in otherwise dull areas.

The quality of light

Those of us living in high latitudes or shaded areas may need extra light, but we must not forget the importance of contrast. Light and shadow, Sun and Moon, morning and evening light all differ in intensity, and their variations add interest. With appropriate use of lighting, we can learn to recreate natural light effects in our home

Direct, reflected, and diffused light all differ in quality. Of the three types, direct light is the strongest. It casts strong shadows and causes glare. Imagine the sunlight in your eyes as you walk or drive east in the early morning sun – this is direct light. Reflected light is softer, bouncing off surfaces in and outside the room, usually importing the tint of the reflected surface. It is the sun shining on a magnolia tree outside a window, turning the room a soft springtime pink. Diffused or filtered light is the softest, and is almost shadowless, since it has passed through a filter such as a screen or a blind. It is evening sunlight seen through the thin walls of a tent.

Remember that direct sunlight bleaches fabric and even paintings. Don't let priceless curtains or rugs be rendered to dust by sunlight! Love the sun in your home, but respect its powers. Hang pictures out of direct light: for instance an art gallery in Edinburgh exhibits its collection of Turner water-colours only in January, when the light is at its weakest.

At home, try to vary the quality of the light according to the function of the room. For instance, kitchens, stairways, and conservatories all need bright, direct light for safety or plant growth. But sitting rooms and dining areas will benefit from softer reflected or diffused lighting to create a gentle, more welcoming atmosphere.

Many older houses still have just one central overhead light per room, which is inflexible as well as very unattractive. Fortunately, we can now choose from a vast array of lighting aids such as uplighters, spotlights, halogen lights, and dimmer controls. Candles can add instant atmosphere, though they need careful monitoring. Low-energy full-spectrum light bulbs (blue and yellow) and tubes are now available to fit into regular domestic light fittings. As well as keeping you alert and responsive and being invaluable to hobbyists, they can also help alleviate common problems such as premenstrual syndrome (PMS).

Ideally, a room should contain several types of lighting for convenience and variety. Work or study areas need spotlights or task lighting, while seating areas can be lit with table or floor lamps for atmosphere. A striking ornament or picture can be illuminated for immediate effect, and dark corners can be rescued from gloom with the help of soft lighting.

Above all, dare to experiment – find the combination of lighting that suits you and your family. Think creatively, and you will rapidly improve the look of your home as well as saving your eyesight.

Light bounces off mirrors and other shiny surfaces in a room, greatly increasing the brightness and giving a feeling of spaciousness. Such decorative devices are ideal in a bathroom, where good lighting is essential (opposite).

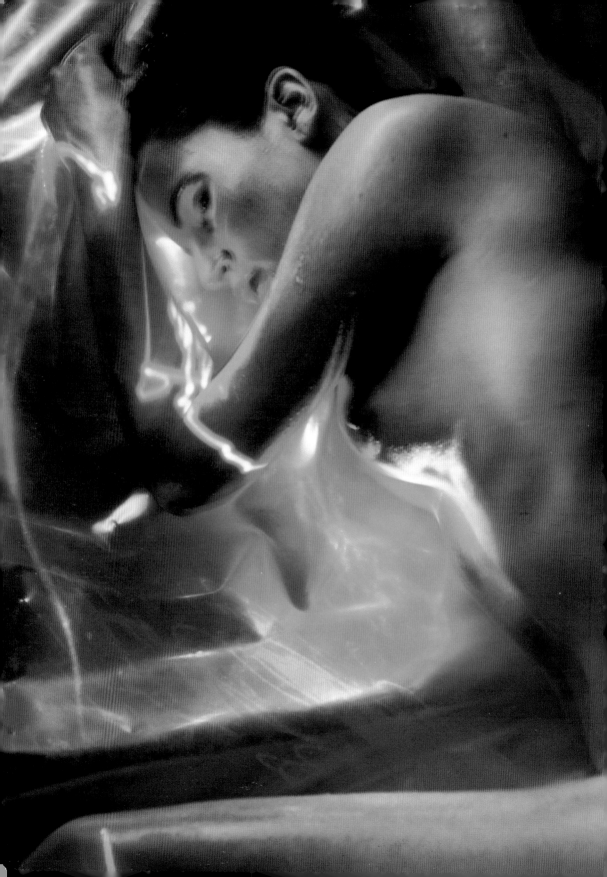

Healing with light

Light is essential for the health of the human body and its immune system. And there is a growing awareness that light, as part of carefully managed therapies, can cure illness. As the pioneer of light therapy, Jacob Liberman says: "The medicine of the future is light. We are healing ourselves with that which is our essence." These new approaches to health make use of the energetic nature of light, vibrational techniques and technologies rather than chemicals to rebalance the body's own endogenous fields and radiations. The central principle of all of these techniques is that disease is the result of the natural vibrational energy that we all emit being altered or unbalanced. Healing is the restoration of this balance.

Not surprisingly, the world's pharmaceutical corporations do not share this view, arguing that only chemical means – pharmaceuticals – can restore health. But this attitude is changing under the influence of increasing evidence to the contrary. In my laboratory we were the first to demonstrate that the viability of the white blood cells, which defend us from infection, is protected by the endogenous electric fields from their owner. By contrast, the endogenous fields from another human being have no protective effect on those cells. Without these endogenous fields, originating in the brain and heart, our bodies soon succumb to infection and disease.

Health could, therefore, be defined as being the state when all the cells of the body are functioning competently and in an organized fashion. The influence that organizes the cells is the endogenous electric field of the organism. Any electric field can be influenced by another, and the electric fields of sunlight have a beneficial influence, provided we select the correct component. Judging from the increased incidence of childhood cancer among populations living near high-voltage powerlines, exposure to the wrong electric fields can have serious consequences.

Auras and light therapy

This photograph was taken by a technique called Polycontrast Interference Photography (PIP), an imaging system invented by British scientist Harry Oldfield. The image reveals the aura, or endogenous field, around the body and has proved to be a valuable aid in diagnosing imbalances in the body.

The notion of the aura is an old-established tenet of energy medicine, with the accompanying dogma that this aura acts as a protective influence which, in certain circumstances, can be penetrated by noxious forces. Mainstream scientists run a mile when they hear words like "aura". Talk to them softly about endogenous fields and they calm down a little, but not much. Explain that the heart's beating is controlled by electric fields, mention the EEG recording of brain rhythms and they may even timidly approach you again.

In 1911 Dr Walter Kilner (who invented the famous Kilner jar for preserving fruit), risked his position as director of the X-ray department of St Thomas's Hospital in London, by publishing an heretical book called *The Human Atmosphere or the Aura made Visible with the Aid of Chemical Screens*. In it he reported that an emanation from human bodies can be seen through specially made spectacles which allowed vision in the ultraviolet part of the spectrum. These had a double screen containing a liquid dye called dicyanin, dissolved in alcohol.

This emanation according to Kilner consisted of three zones:
• A thin dark layer close to the skin
• A vaporous layer with rays pointing away from the skin
• A tenuous outer layer about 15 centimetres (6 inches) across, with varying density and colours.

Kilner found that these layers varied according to age, sex, mental energy, and health state. He went so far as to use them tentatively to diagnose diseases such as hepatitis, appendicitis, cancer, epilepsy, and psychological states. One can still buy Kilner glasses today, even on the Internet, but their use in mainstream medicine is nonexistent.

My hypothesis is that what used to be called the aura is in fact the body's endogenous field. Proving the existence of the body's endogenous field and its function in a way acceptable to normal science is not so easy. In our laboratory, my wife

Tamara, a microbiologist, and I have managed to do this with an experiment which, as I write, is being replicated in several other institutions.

A revolutionary experiment

Every living creature gives out a cocktail of electromagnetic radiations, and human beings are no exception. It makes sense that UV is part of those radiations because UV can destroy noxious bacteria. Clearly, if the level of UV emitted falls, the bacteria (and other noxious agents) have a better chance of taking a hold on the body's defences.

In our experiment, we took a small amount of peripheral blood from a donor and isolated the white blood cells, or lymphocytes, which are responsible for protecting the body from infection. These we kept in a culture, but we divided the culture into three separate identical phials. In one of the phials we placed a gold wire, the end of which was attached to the donor's skin surface. One of the other two phials also had a gold wire, but this was sealed into the phial, and the third phial contained only the culture. All three were encased in a small metal box to keep out other stray radiations, and this box was taped to the donor's arm overnight.

The next day we found that the cells that had been able to receive signals down the gold wire from the donor were significantly more viable than those in the other two phials. We repeated this experiment more than a dozen times, always with the same result. When we tried connecting someone other than the donor to the phials, the effect disappeared. The donor's endogenous fields, radiating from the skin surface but probably more powerful inside the body, were unique to that person, just like DNA, and no other person's signals had the protective effect we had discovered.

Thus we were the first scientists to show unequivocally that the viability of the white blood cells that protect us against infection is itself protected by the endogenous electric fields of the cells' owner. The endogenous fields from another human being had no protective effect on those cells. Each person's endogenous fields protected only his or her own white blood cells. Our experiment eliminated any possibility that chemical or even magnetic fields were responsible for the protective effect. Only the electric fields were responsible. From this, it is reasonable to argue that multicellular health is the result of endogenous field influences rather than simply the result of ingesting any materials such as pharmaceuticals. Without these endogenous fields, originating in the brain and heart, maybe even from the cells themselves, our bodies would soon succumb to infection and disease, at least part of which is electromagnetically engendered.

Healing with light

Gamma rays, X-rays, and ultraviolet, as well as visible light and high-energy cosmic radiation, come from sunlight. When one considers this scattered cocktail of radiations reaching us from the Sun, it is reasonable to suggest that we need to use specific parts of light in order to carry out specific healing functions. In recognition of this, a large variety of therapeutic instruments has evolved which are used to apply light and near-light frequencies selectively.

One simple instrument is a device called the LightMask developed by Dr David Noton at Hammersmith Hospital in London. The mask looks similar to the sleep masks issued on aeroplanes, except that it contains flickering red lights.

When worn for 15 to 30 minutes a day the mask has proved to be extremely effective in the treatment of migraine and premenstrual syndrome (PMS). The results of Noton's study with the LightMask on PMS were reported in the *Journal of Obstetrics and Gynaecology* in 1998. PMS sufferers were treated with the LightMask for three months. Of the 17 women in the trial, 12 no longer suffered PMS by the end of that time,

The LightMask, which shines flickering lights directly into the eyes, has proved to be an effective treatment for premenstrual syndrome (PMS) and migraine. Research shows that in PMS sufferers the body's internal clock becomes disrupted from the normal external rhythms of day and night. The mask's light appears to help the clock to re-synchronize.

three more showed improvement, one dropped out, and the last showed no change. A similar study on migraine patients had equally dramatic results.

Anther recent development is a device named the Photron. This issues a gently flickering, coloured strobe light into the patient's eyes, using the colour appropriate to the treatment. For recent post-traumatic stress conditions, such as wartime experiences or car accident, calm colours like green or blue have been found to be most effective, whereas for deep or distant trauma orange and yellow are preferable.

Syntonics

This technique, using coloured filtered light, has been shown to improve a patient's visual field and can also benefit the immune system and emotional state. It was developed by an American scientist, Dr Harry Riley Spitler. Spitler's approach was to treat the body by way of the eyes, thereby using the shortest pathway to the brain. His research showed that different colours of light entering the eyes can affect the balance of the body and its functions.

During the 1920s in his work on light therapy, Dr Spitler conducted experiments on rabbits, which he kept on the same regimens and in identical cages but exposed to different coloured lighting. Certain lighting caused abnormalities in the rabbits and he concluded that although heredity and environment are major factors in health, light can also alter function, behaviour and physiological response. Accordingly, in 1927, Spitler began to develop the first light-dispensing instruments for ocular application. He called his new system "Syntonics", from the word "syntony" meaning to balance, because it brought the autonomic system into balance.

Spitler's College of Syntonic Optometry still flourishes today, some 70 years later, with hundred of US practitioners, as well as others in Australia and Europe. In a Syntonics treatment, the patient sits in a darkened room in front of a fixed lamp that delivers coloured light of specific frequencies. A treatment lasts about 20 minutes and is generally repeated once a day for about three weeks.

One of the more spectacular applications of Syntonics comes from the finding that unsuspected visual loss limits learning capacity and that 69 per cent of children with reading problems have a measurable enlargement of the blind spot, where the optic nerve leaves the retina. Twenty minutes daily treatment with yellow-green light and then ruby light can bring dramatic improvements in auditory memory as well as in the eyesight itself.

Cleansing light

Light is also a powerful bactericide as the work of Downes and Blunt demonstrated (see page 92). In the 1930s Emmitt Knott and a medical colleague, Virgil Hancock, pioneered the idea of using a converted Hanovia water-cooled UV lamp for the purpose of irradiating blood. Bacterially infected blood was cleaned by this process and then returned to the body. The technique was spectacularly successful.

Syntonics was the first therapy that treated the patient by shining light directly into the eyes (opposite). A Syntonics treatment can not only improve the patient's vision but also boost the immune system.

Jaundice in newborn babies is caused by the accumulation of a bile pigment called bilirubin in the blood. It is very common and generally clears up in a few days, but some babies may need phototherapy treatment (overleaf). The baby is placed in an incubator and exposed to blue light. This breaks down the bilirubin, which then passes out of the body in the urine.

I followed their exciting literature through until about 1950, reading of thousands of success stories in cases of septicemia where all else had failed, when, after some critical papers, the technique disappeared in the wake of antibiotic medicine. Now when some antibiotics no longer work because the bugs have become resistant, hemo-irradiation is back again. In St Petersburg, Professor Kira Samoilova, head of photobiology at the Russian Academy of Sciences, claims success in treating lung, intestinal, and breast cancers, stomach ulcers, and so on. The Food and Drug Administration in the USA has approved the use of blood irradiation for the treatment of infectious diseases in 120 clinics. In the treatment about 5 percent of the blood in the body is passed through the irradiating device once or twice a day for as long as necessary.

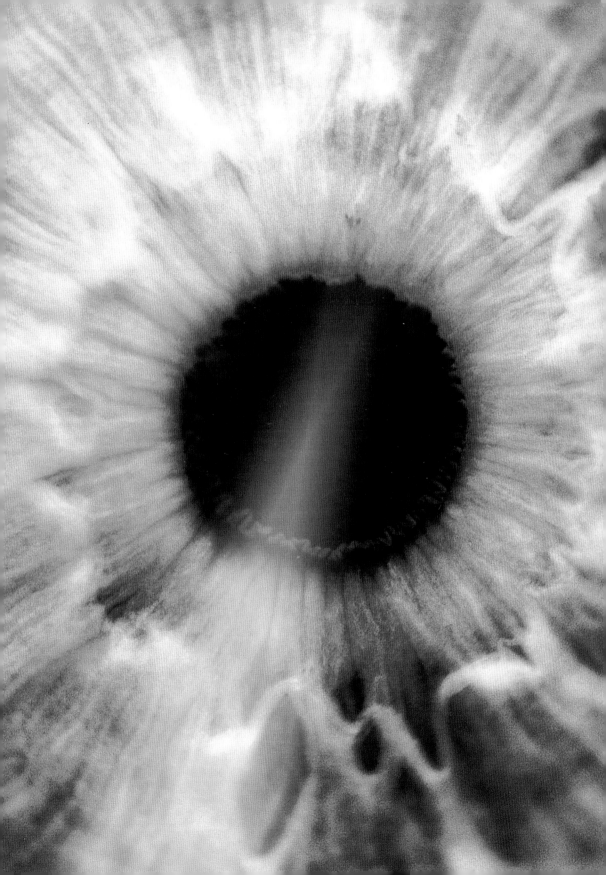

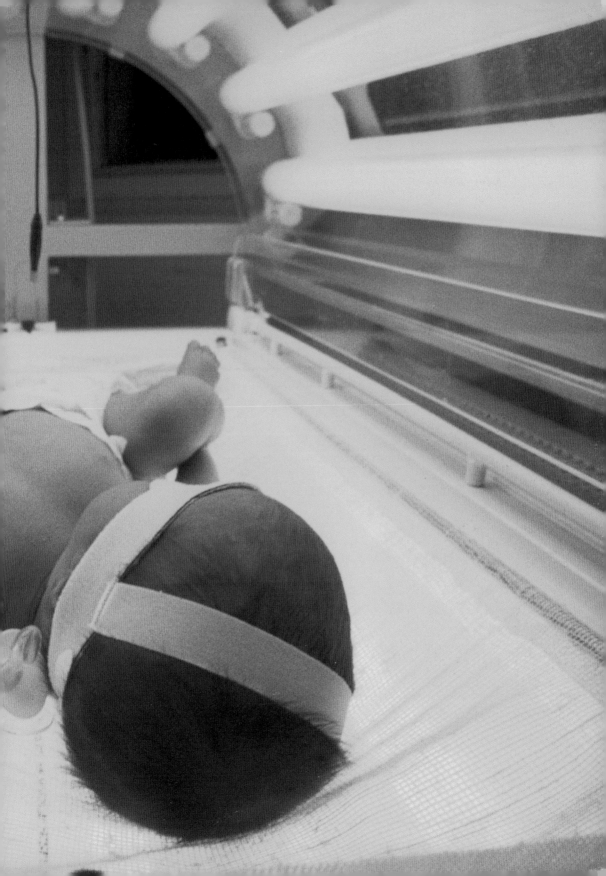

Messages in light beams

When we think of sunlight, we imagine it coming to us in straight lines, like the shafts of sunlight in a leafy glade. As we walk into the sunlight it can also dazzle us because the light is unpolarized and arrives at all angles. But if a thin grid of bars is placed between the source and the eyes, the Sun's glare disappears because the light has been polarized: only rays of one plane are now reaching the eyes. Some sunglasses rely on this principle to protect the eyes from glare. The discovery of polarized light is by no means new – any electromagnetic radiation can be polarized.

Two scientists, John Stephenson from Surrey in southeast England and Dr Marta Fenyo of Budapest, have discovered how to exploit this phenomenon of polarized light for health. They use a combination of polarized light and full-spectrum lighting, which aims to mimic the frequencies of natural sunlight. Ministry of Defence trials on this Virtual Daylight system discovered that it could produce a 70 percent drop in headaches, eye fatigue, and VDU vision problems.

But that is only part of the story. Dr Fenyo had discovered many years before that polarized light can also boost immune system responses and cure conditions such as leg ulcers. At the National Institute of Radiobiology in Budapest, Dr Fenyo and a colleague, Dr Tamara Kubasova, tested polarized light on mice by an indirect method. They took some serum from tumour-bearing mice, which had been successfully treated with polarized light, and injected the serum into other mice with tumours. The injected mice recovered, proving that the polarizing effect could be transferred simply via the serum.

Encouraged, Dr Fenyo tried a different technique: this time with dogs dying of cancer. She took some blood from the animals, irradiated it with polarized light and then reinjected the blood into the animals. There was a dramatic reduction in tumour size, accompanied by a remarkable increase in alertness in the dogs. The list of ailments successfully treated with

The polarized light emitted by the Bioptron device (above) activates and regenerates the body's cells. This boosts the immune system and helps the body to rebalance and heal itself. The Bioptron has proved extremely effective in the treatment of severe burns.

polarized light continues to increase: mastitis in cattle, acne, sports injuries, psoriasis. Altogether some 20,000 patients have received her polarized light therapy.

A version of this technique uses a tool called the Bioptron, which uses visible incoherent polarized (VIP) light. The Bioptron is used for treating conditions such as acne, herpes simplex, and external hemorrhoids. During treatment, light, comprising visible cold light and part of the infrared spectrum, is shone on the affected area for between two to six minutes. Treatment should be administered once or twice daily until the condition improves.

The light works by instigating a sort of chain reaction. It increases the activity of the cell membrane, which in turn boosts cell production of enzymes and energy reserves. At the same time, the body tissues become capable of absorbing more oxygen. This results in stimulation of the immune system and a strengthening of immune responses.

BICOM and bioresonance therapy

At the Hippocampus Research Institute in Budapest, Gabor Lednyiczky and his colleagues have also been researching ways of using the body's own natural fields for healing purposes. The capacity for health fails when serious damage occurs in the communications pathways of any organism, claims Lednyiczky. At Hippocampus, they have developed an instrument called the Cerebellum Multifunction Medical Instrument (CMMI) which diagnoses the state of the patient from a variety of aspects, such as amino acids, proteins, lipids, enzymes and hormones, by means of their electrical signals.

By analysing this information, the scientists claim they can feed back corrective signals from a device called the BICOM to correct the anomaly. The general approach is now called bioresonance therapy, or BRT and the BICOM machine is manufactured by the Brügemann Institute in Germany. The idea behind the technique is that since the patient's own oscillations, or signals, are electromagnetic in nature, they can be picked up from the patient's body using electrodes containing a specially prepared magnetic foil which has a field strength similar to that of the Earth.

The BICOM filters out the frequencies that are known to be harmonious in order to identify those that are anomalous. A feedback system via another electrode then enhances the harmonious and attenuates the disharmonious frequencies by inversion – the peaks of the patient's disharmonious waves are converted into their equivalent troughs and fed back into the patient. The frequencies involved are very high, right up to the UV range of some 30 nanometre wavelengths, and hence include visible light.

Hans Brügemann recognizes that the human body is an open system, with energy entering and leaving all the time. He points out that the physicist G. B. Kirchhoff (1824–87) discovered that at 37° Celsius (98.4°F) radiation in (absorption) equals radiation out (emission). In other words, the body is continuously emitting and absorbing energy. And at the same time we have our own unique and vitally important energy system in operation.

Obviously incoming and outgoing radiation must be equal to maintain thermal equilibrium, and since the human body is constantly burning nutrients we would perish through overheating if isolated from the outside world.

The balance of the more subtle flows of energy also has to be maintained. We need the inflow of sunlight, and of specific frequencies within sunlight, if we are to stay in good health. Conversely, the artificial energies of electricity, to which we are not attuned by evolution, have harmful effects. Not surprisingly, acupuncture points, which are pathways for energy flows, have been found to conduct light into the body.

Rebalancing the body

Another such rebalancing approach is Biolumanetics. The system was developed by Patrick Richards, who in 1983 designed a device he called a Luminator, which balances air temperatures from floor to ceiling and from wall to wall for efficient energy management in offices. He found that after its installation the office staff begun reporting that their general health had improved, including the reduction of lower back pain and migraine headaches. On further investigation, Richards discovered that, as well as balancing the temperature in the room, the Luminator altered the magnetic field and changed the available light in the room from incoherent (light going in all directions) to coherent, or polarized, light.

Further research uncovered the astonishing fact that light from living organisms could be imaged in the Luminator's field. It is this particular aspect of the Luminator that is used in Biolumanetics. All living things emit light and a healthy person emits brighter, more coherent light than an unhealthy one. Diagnosis in Biolumanetics begins with the client being photographed in a room containing the Luminator by an imaging technique called VRIC (Visual Reference of Image Coherence). The photo may show the subject as blurred, revealing a loss of vitality or coherence in that person. The therapist then attempts to improve that vitality. Whatever solution or cream is suggested as a remedy for the problem is given to the patient to hold while he or she is photographed again. If the remedy is correct, the image will be dramatically sharper, more coherent, showing an improvement in vitality and rebalancing the body. The remedy is thus proved to be suitable even before it has been used by the client.

One of the most interesting uses of Biolumanetics therapy is in relationship problems. A woman suffering severe stress, for example, may be photographed holding pictures of different members of her family. Her "coherence" or the light she emanates may appear dramatically different with each one, perhaps revealing hidden difficulties in family dynamics.

This series of pictures of a Biolumanetics client shows that the coherence of her image improves when she holds the correct remedy for her condition (bottom).

A dome of light

In her centre at Kew in London, Thrity Engineer maintains one of the world's ten Monocrom Light Domes. She operates it in combination with Biolumanetics and the Luminator, in an integrated system she calls 3S (scientific, subtle and sacred). The dome is the brainchild of Swedish architect and therapist Karl Ryberg, with whom she trained. The dome uses mono-chromatic light – light in a very narrow bandwidth of about 700 nanometres. The light is pure – monochromatic green, for example, is not a mixture of blue and yellow but a pure green, similar to laser light.

The dome is a white structure, about 3 metres (10 feet 6 inches) high. The client, dressed in an unbleached cotton robe, steps into the dome and lies down. The doorway is sealed and the experience begins. Monochromatic light is beamed into the dome via a powerful projector lamp and plays through all colours of the spectrum. The therapist may control the colours used or allow patients to select their own colours, depending on the type of condition being treated and its seriousness. The dome shape makes proportions seem infinite so clients feel as though they are floating in a world of colour. The eyes cannot focus because there is nothing to focus on, the brain pulses slow and the brain reaches a calmer, *alpha* state. A normal session lasts 15 minutes and three or four weeks should elapse between sessions.

The Monocrom Light Dome is an effective treatment for many disorders, including stress. This patient was photographed by Biofeedback imaging before treatment in the dome (above) and shortly afterwards (opposite). Clearly a dramatic change has taken place, but this change is at an innate rather than a conscious level.

Research at the Laser Biology Institute in Moscow has shown that monochromatic light reaches the very nucleus of the cells and so wakes up the body at the deepest cellular level. Treatment in the dome has been shown to be extremely effective for phobias, depression, SAD and other stress-related disorders. It can also be a deeply pleasurable and uplifting experience. I speculate that only the frequencies needed by the body are absorbed by the skin, but by providing the entire visible spectrum in the same way as full-spectrum lighting, any frequencies not available before can be absorbed, thereby rebalancing the body's energy.

Photodynamic therapy

One of the most exciting light treatments is photodynamic therapy, or PDT, proven to be highly successful in treating certain types of cancers. It is also used to treat skin ailments such as acne and eczema.

PDT utilizes porphyrins, a light-sensitizing component of hemoglobin. These porphyrins have an iron atom inside the nitrogen square and are the means by which we can carry oxygen, attached to the iron atom, around our body for delivery to respiring tissues. Why oxygen? Because oxygen can accept the unwanted electrons left over after the process of energy synthesis is carried out within cells. Otherwise, the electrons, in the form of unpaired free radicals, might upset our other cells and damage them. So porphyrins play an important subsidiary role in energy creation, both in plants and animals.

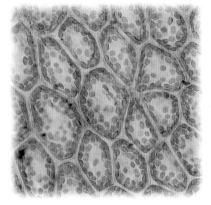

A plant's green leaves contain chlorophyll, which uses sunlight to make sugar (sucrose), with oxygen as a by-product. The chlorophyll strongly absorbs red and blue light, but not green, which is reflected. The part of the chlorophyll that absorbs red and blue is a molecule structured with four nitrogens forming a square. Inside the square an atom of magnesium is trapped – an arrangement called a porphyrin. It is the porphyrins in chlorophyll that convert light into electrical energy.

When the respiration process of cells goes wrong, they can become cancerous. Normally, energy in the form of adenosine triphosphate (ATP), the energy molecule of nearly all living creatures, is created by organelles called mitochondria inside our cells in a process known as oxidative phosphorylation (the "ox-phos" metabolic pathway). This simply means that the process adds a phosphate to adenosine diphosphate (ADP), and uses oxygen as an electron "dustbin" or final electron acceptor for the spare electrons.

If any carcinogen blocks this amazingly efficient energy machine, the cell in desperation turns to a more primitive means of making energy, glycolysis. By this it can only make a third as many ATP molecules from glucose as it did before, 12 instead of 35 to be precise. So the cell can stay alive, but only just, because nearly all its reduced energy goes into maintaining the essential pumps that maintain the integrity of its plasma membrane, or "skin". About 40 percent of the energy made by a cell's mitochondria goes into keeping the plasma membrane intact.

Now the poor cell has a desperate choice: either to stay like that, half dead, or to obtain increased supplies of glucose and make more energy. The easiest way to make more energy is to resorb the sugar-candy sticks on its plasma membrane surface called glycoproteins. But these glycoproteins are its signal transduction means, telling the cell what is happening in the outside world, so the cell then becomes blind to instructions from other cells or from the brain's controlling signals. This in turn means it no longer behaves as part of the body, but abandons regulatory growth control, and may start to divide unregulated, no longer controlled by the body's genetic electric fields.

That this is so is confirmed by three facts. First, cancer cells almost always have no glycoproteins on their plasma membrane surfaces. Second, they do not obey the rules of normal contact inhibition (when normal cells touch any other cell they stop dividing). And third, cancer cells are intensely glucose hungry. It is this problem in cancer that is being tackled today by photodynamic therapy (PDT).

The pioneer of PDT

In PDT, cancer cells are bombarded with light at specific frequencies in the red frequency range, in combination with light-sensitive porphyrins. PDT was pioneered by Thomas Dougherty, a research chemist at Roswell Park Memorial Institute in Buffalo, New York. He extracted porphyrins from hemoglobin, the oxygen-capturing molecules that fill our red blood cells.

Blood owes its red colour to an iron atom at the heart of its porphyrin ring. Shining red light at this molecule causes it to vibrate in resonance. Depending on the intensity used, the vibration may well work to kick start the cancer cell back to its normal ox-phos pathway, abandoning the inefficient glycolysis means of ATP synthesis. Another theory is that the singlet oxygen, produced when the porphyrins are exposed to

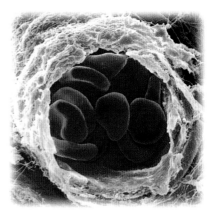

Red blood cells are full of hemoglobin molecules, each of which contains an iron atom. Oxygen attaches to the iron atoms and is carried round the body in the blood.

red ruby laser light at higher intensities, is lethal to the half-dead, half-alive, out-of-control cancer cells.

By offering an alternative electron-accepting mechanism in the form of the vibrated porphyrins, singlet oxygen is introduced, and the cancer cells may be encouraged to revert to their ordinary oxygen-using pathways and return to normal regulatory growth control. The same vibratory approach helps the cell expel its waste products and take in the nutrients it needs; hence there are applications for photodynamic light therapy beyond cancer alone.

Since its beginnings in the 1970s, PDT has been refined and it is now administered via soft ruby laser light and fibre optics. The list of cancers successfully treated with PDT is impressive and includes advanced lung, oesophogeal, head and neck, and pituitary cancers, skin tumours, and some gynecological conditions. Post-surgical use of PDT can also mop up malignant cells left over after surgical excision of brain tumours.

A PDT treatment

Employing light of a specific frequency in the red part of the light spectrum is a recognition that vibratory medicine works at a distance and without chemicals. In a PDT treatment, the patient is first injected intravenously with a photosensitive chemical called DHE, or Photofrin. The chemical is allowed to circulate for a time, while the patient is protected from bright lights or sunlight. The chemical congregates in cancer tissue, as well as in other parts of the body such as the kidneys, but after a day or so clears from these other areas, and the light treatment can then be applied. This uses specifically tuned red light with a frequency of 630 nanometres. It is delivered by an argon-pumped laser, via a hair-thin fibre optic filament, directly to the affected area. Within hours of the treatment, the cancer cells begin to die, but the normal tissue of the body is unaffected.

The Paterson lamp (opposite) is used for treating skin cancer by photodynamic therapy. First, a cream containing Photofrin is applied and this is taken up by the cancer cells. The red light, specifically tuned to 630 nanometres, activates the Photofrin, which then kills the cancer cells.

Healing energies

Researchers are also working on ways of delivering light-energy radiation directly to affected tissues via machines using "excited" gem substances such as diamond and sapphire.

An English electronics engineer Jon Whale has designed a machine called the Lux Caduceus III, which uses electronics transducers incorporating emerald and blue sapphire components. The machine has been used with great success in the treatment of psoriasis and cystitis. The essence of the concept is that light can be imbued with the characteristics of the gems at a quantum level, and that our bodies can sense this at a subliminal level.

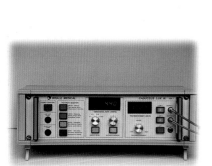

Jon Whale's electronic gem lamp therapy has proved successful in the treatment of disease and injury. Gems deep inside a chamber in each lamp are electronically excited by a precision electronic instrument (above). The frequencies used promote rapid healing

In electronic gem lamp therapy, light is shone on the appropriate area of the body for 10 to 20 minutes. This patient is being treated for stress (opposite).

Focused, filtered light is beamed on to the patient from the machine, which contains gems in the path of the light. Just as your hand is clearly irradiated right through by an electric torch (you can see this at any time in the dark), so the beams from the high-intensity bulbs in this machine will penetrate deep into the body tissues. Whale's patients have recovered from breast lumps, arthritis, eczema, and other disorders.

Colour therapist Theo Gimbel offers a torch, which shines through a crystal needle in a somewhat similar way. His instrument, the CoCrysto torch, uses filters rather than gems, but the oxides incorporated in these filters are the same as one might find in a gem. Wear something white, hold the torch 2.5 centimetres (1 inch) away from the body and focus it on the chakras. The effect will depend on which chakra is awakened, but the consequences can be powerful.

The Eye Healing Lamp

Theo Gimbel has also designed a lamp for healing cataracts, glaucoma, and other severe eye disturbances. It is also said to improve long and short sight by mobilizing the muscles of the iris. The Eye Healing lamp (see page 150) incorporates red or turquoise filters, depending on the condition, and can be used at home under instruction.

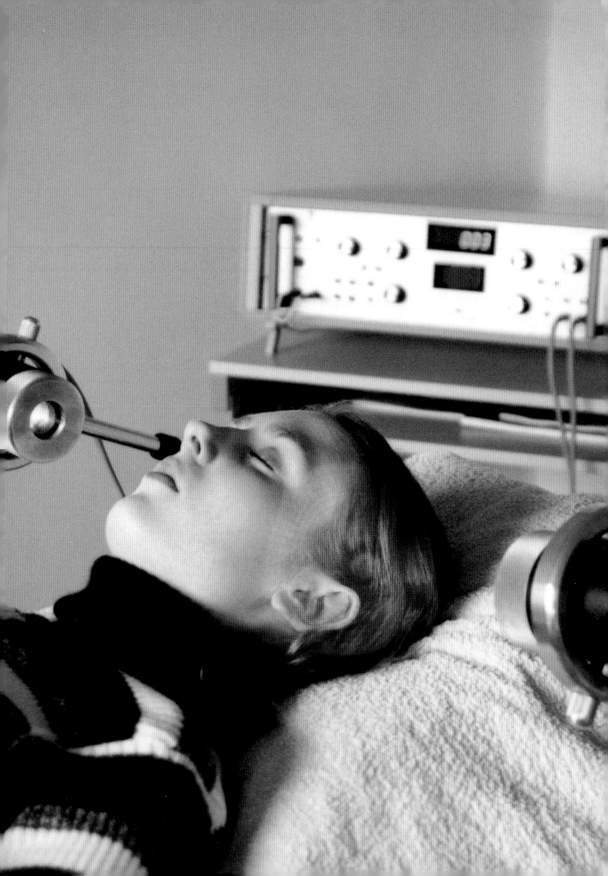

The power of infrared

The far infrared part of the spectrum has unusual physical properties: it is a well-known physical phenomenon that infrared radiation is generated by vibration and rotation of atoms and molecules in any substance with a temperature above absolute zero. Infrared radiation is sometimes wrongly known as heat radiation because it generates heat in any absorbing object in its path. However, so do light rays, X-rays, and even high-intensity radar beams. Because the IR band falls between the bands of light and radio, it demonstrates many of the characteristics of both visible light and radar waves. It may be focused by lenses, yet can be transmitted like radar through materials that block visible light.

The use of far infrared for health by means of a new material called photon platinum has largely escaped the West so far, but in Japan, where it was invented, it is now in widespread use for improving the skin. The material, which feels strangely warm to the touch and looks like cotton wool or medical gauze, is composed of trillions of tiny particles of platinum rod embedded in a nylon polymer. Any kind of energy activates it by causing electrons to follow the easiest pathways up and down the platinum micro-rods. This in turn produces radiation in the far infrared region, with wavelengths of 4–14

microns. Since this length range is the same as the diameter of most organic cells, it has a resonant effect on cells and assists the passage of nutrients and waste products through their plasma membranes. A face mask incorporating photon platinum improves the skin by encouraging the growth of underlying new cells and sloughing away of old, dirty cells. The material is also used for treating cellulite.

Jacob Liberman, pioneer of light therapy

It is a fitting end to this chapter to pay homage to Jacob Liberman, a pioneer in the use of light therapy. Liberman, born in 1947, gained a degree in optometry at the University of Georgia, and a PhD in 1986. His research and his 1991 book *Light: Medicine of the Future* has inspired the development of a whole profession of light therapy.

The benefits of light therapy can be dramatic. As Jacob Liberman said, "Our task is to take in light so that we may merge with our true selves and our destiny, thus facilitating the healing of our planet. As each of us becomes whole we radiate light – light from within – unimpeded by our self-imposed emotional and physical blocks." Armed with these insights, you may be about to change forever.

During strenuous exercise, lactic acid can build up in the muscles, making it impossible to carry on. Photon platinum can delay this build-up and increase energy output substantially. Olympic cyclists (below) tested shorts incorporating photon platinum and found a noticeable improvement in their performance.

Bibliography

Birren, F., *Colour Psychology and Colour Healing*, Citadel Press, Secaucus, NJ, 1961

Brennan, Barbara Ann, *Hands of Light*, Bantam Books, New York, 1987

Brügemenn, Hans (ed.), *Bioresonance and multiresonance therapy (BRT)*, Vol 1, Haug International, Brussels, 1993

Clark, L., *Ancient Art of Colour Therapy*, Pocket Books, New York, 1975

Coghill, Roger and Oldfield, Harry, *The Dark Side of the Brain*, Element Books, Dorset, 1988 and Element Books, Boston, 1988

Coghill, Roger, *Something in the Air*, Coghill Research Laboratories, Pontypool, Gwent, 1999

Collis, John Stewart, *The Vision of Glory*, Penguin Books, Middlesex, 1975.

Cousens, Gabriel, *Spiritual Nutrition and the Rainbow Diet*, Cassandra Press, Boulder CO, 1986

Devin-Adair Co., *Health and Light*, Old Greenwich CT, 1973

Dinshah, Darius, *Let there be Light* Dinshah Health Society, Malaga, NJ, 1985

Gerber, Richard, *Vibrational Medicine*, Bear and Co., Santa Fe, New Mexico, 1988

Gimbel, Theo, *Healing with Colour*, Gaia Books, London, 1997

Gimbel, Theo, *Healing with Colour and Light*, Fireside, New York, 1998

Hollwich, F., *The influence of ocular light perception on metabolism in man*, Springer Verlag, New York, 1979

Hunt, Roland, *The Seven Keys to Colour Healing*, Harper and Row, San Francisco, 1971

Kaplan, Robert-Michael, *Seeing beyond 20/20*, Beyond Words Publishing, Hillsboro, OR, 1987

Kime, Z., *Sunlight*, World health publications, Penryn, CA, 1980

Liberman, Jacob, *Light: Medicine of the Future*, Bear and Co. Publishing, Santa Fe, New Mexico, 1991

Mayer, E., *Clinical applications of sunlight and artificial radiation*, Williams and Wilkins Co, Baltimore, 1926

McKenzie, T.C. and King, A.A., *Practical Ultraviolet Light therapy*, Ernest Benn Ltd., London (1926)

Ott, John, *Health and Light*, The Devin-Adair Co., Greenwich, CT, 1973

Ott, John, *Light Radiation and You*, The Devin-Adair Co., Greenwich, CT, 1982

Pearson, David, *New Natural House Book*, Conran Octopus, London, 1998 and Fireside, New York, 1998

Pearson, David, *The Natural House Catalog*, Simon & Schuster, New York, 1996

Popp, Fritz Albert, Warnke, Ulrich et al, *Electromagnetic Bio-Information*, Urban and Schwanenberg, Munich, 1989

Reiter, Russel J. and Robinson, Jo, *Melatonin*, Bantam Books, New York, 1995

Rosenthal, Norman, *Seasons of the Mind*, Bantam Books, New York, 1989

Scott-Mumby, Keith, *Virtual Medicine*, Thorsons, London, 1999

Simpson, Liz, *The Book of Crystal Healing*, Gaia Books, London, 1997 and Sterling, New York, 1997

Soyka, Fred and Edmonds, Alan, *The Ion Effect*, Bantam Books, New York, 1977

Steiner, Rudolf, *Colour*, Rudolf Steiner Press, London, 1982

Szent-Gyorgy, Albert, *Introduction to a Submolecular Biology*, Academic Press New York, 1960

Szent-Gyorgy, Albert, *Bioenergetics*, Morrow, New York, (1957)

Szent-Gyorgyi, Albert, *Bioelectronics*, Academic Press, New York, 1968

Tompkins, Peter and Bird, Christopher, *The Secret Life of Plants*, Harper and Row, New York, 1973

Wood, Betty, *The Healing Power of Colour*, Destiny Books, New York, 1984

Wortman, Richard, Baum, Michael et al, *The Medical and Biological Effects of Light*, New York Academy of Sciences, New York, 1985

The Principles of Light and Colour, Citadel Press, Secaucus, NJ, 1967

References

A selection of milestone references for the scientifically inclined reader.

R. ALTSCHUL. & I.H. HERMAN
Ultraviolet radiation and chlolesterol metabolism *Procs. 7th Ann. Mtg. Amer. Soc. for study of Arteriosclerosis* In: Circulation 8438 (1953)

R.B. ANDERSON, J.E. ROSENBLITH
Light Sensitivity in the Neonate. *Biologica Neonat.* 7: 83 (1964)

V.N. ANISIMOV, O.V. ZHUKOVA
Effect of the light regime and electromagnetic fields on carcinogenesis of the mammary gland in female rats *Biophysics* Vol 41 No 4: pp.817-823 (1996)

I.I. BELYAYEV et al
Combined use of UV radiation to control acute respiratory disease. *Vestn. Akad. Med. Nauk. SSSR* 3: 37 (1975)

VALERI BERAL, S. EVANS et al
Malignant Melanoma and exposure to fluorescent lighting at work. *Lancet* 2. pp.290-293 (August, 1982)

C. BETANCUR, G. DELL' OMO, E. ALLERA
Magnetic field effects on stress-induced analgesia in mice: Modulation of light. *Neurosci. Lett.* 182: 147-150 (1994)

F. BALDERREY, OTGAR BARKUS
Influence of light energy (sunlight) on the hydrogen ion concentration of the blood. *Am. Rev. Tuberc.* 9: 107 (1924)

H.F. BLUM
Sulfanilomide and increased senstivity to light *Am. J. Physiol.* 129: 312 (1940)

R.J. CREMER, P.W. PERRMAN
Influence of light on hyperbilirubinemia in infants. *Lancet* I (1958) p. 1094

C.A. CZEISLER, J.S. ALLEN et al
(2-29a) Bright Light resets the human circadian pacemaker independent of the timing of the sleep wake cycle. *Science* 223: 667-671 (1986)

T.J. DOUGHERTY et al
Photoradiation therapy II: cure of animal tumours with hematoporphyrin and light. *J. Natl. Cancer Inst.* 55: 115 (1975)

A. DOWNES, A. and T.P. BLUNT
Researches on the the effect of light upon bacteria and other organisms. *Proc. Roy. Soc.* 26: 488-500 (1877)

T.H. EAMES
Restrictions of the visual field as a handicap to learning. *J. Educ. Res.* 19: 460-463 (February 1936)

W.F. GANONG et al
Penetration of light into the brains of mammals. *Endocr,* 72:962-963, (1963)

D.T. HARRIS
Effects of UV light on oxygen transport. *Biochem. J.* 20: 280,271 (1926)

W.N. HESS
Reactions to Light in the Earthworm. *J. of Morph.* 39: 515-423 (1924)

W.N. HESS
Nervous System of the Earthworm. *J. of Morph.* 40: 235-60 (1925)

L. HILL
The physiological effects of light. *Proc. Roy. Soc. Med.* 1923

M.F. HOLICK et al
The photobiosynthesis and metabolism and Vitamin D. *Fed. Proc.* 37: 2567 (1978)

F. HOLLWICH, B. DIECKHAUS
Endocrine system and blindness. *German Medical Monthly* 1: (1971c) p22

F. HOLLWICH, B. DIECKHUES
The effect of natural and artificial light via the eye on the hormonal and metabolic balance of animal and man. *Ophthalmologica* 180(4): 188-197 (1980)

H. IRLEN
Successful treatment of learning disabilities. *Procs. 91st. Ann Conv. Amer. Psychological Soc.* Anaheim, CA (August 1983)

J.R. JOHNSON
The effect of carbon arc radiation on blood pressure and cardiac output. *Amer. J. Physiol.* 114: 594 (1935)

T.J. KARU, O.A. TIPHLOVA et al
Stimulation of *E. coli* growth by laser and incoherent red light. *Nuovo cimento* 2d, 1138-1144. (1983)

T.I. KARU
Photobiological Fundamentals of Low Power Laser Therapy. *IEEE J. of Quantum Electronics.* Vol Pe23 - No 10 (October 1987)

D.F. KRIPKE
Therapeutic effects of bright light in depression. *Ann. NY Acad. Sci.* 453: 270-281 (1985)

L.A. KUNITSINA et al
Therapeutic action of UV irradiation in a complex treatment of patients with intial cerebral atherosclerosis. *Sov. Med.* 33: 89 (1970)

R.W. LAM
Seasonal Affective disorder present-
ing as chronic fatigue syndrome.
Can. J. Psychiatr. 36(9): 680-682
(1991)

A.J. LEWY, T.A. WEHR et al
Light suppresses melatonin secretion
in humans. *Science* 210: 1267-1269
(1980)

J. LIBERMAN
The effect of Syntonic coloured
light stimulation on certain visual
and cognitive functions.
J. Optometric Vision Development 17,
June 1986

J. LOPIPARO
Phototherapy: will colour be the
next medical frontier? *The
Osteopathic Physician* July 1978,
pp.36-39

J.R. LUCEY
Neonatal jaundice and phototherapy
Pediatric Clinics of North America 19
(4) 1-7 (1972)

E. MAYER
Present status of light therapy. *JAMA*
98: 221-230 (1932)

S.F. MCDONALD
Effect of visible light waves on
arthritic pain: a controlled study. *Intl.
J. Biosoc. Res.* 3(2): 49-54 (1982)

GEORGE MILEY
The Knott Technic of Ultraviolet
blood irradiation in acute pyogenic
infections. *NYS J. Med.* 142: 38-46
(1942)

G.P. MILEY, R.E. SEIDEL et al
Ultraviolet blood irradiation therapy
of apparently intractable bronchial
asthma. *Arch. Phys. Med.* Jan 1948:
24-29 91948)

G.P. MILEY, ELMER E. REBBECK
The Knott Technik of Ultraviolet
blood irradiation as a control of
infection in peritonitis. *Rev.
Gastroenterol.* 10: 1-26 (1943)

G. MILEY, J.A. CHRISTENSON
UV blood irradiation therapy -
Further studies in acute infections.
Am. J. Surg. 47: 486-493 (1947)

G. MILEY, J. CHRISTENSEN
Ultraviolet Blood irradiation in
acute virus and virus-type infections.
Rev. Gastroenterol 15 (4): 271-279
(1948)

R.Y. MOORE, A. HELLER et al
Visual pathway mediating pineal
response to environmental light.
Science 155: 220-223 (1967)

R.Y. MOORE, DAVID KLEIN
Visual pathways and the central
neural control of a circadian rhythm
in pineal serotonin N-acetyltrans-
ferase activity. *Brain Res.* 71: 17-33
(1974)

R.M. NEER et al
Stimulation by artificial lighting of
calcium absorption in elderly human
subjects. *Nature* 229: 255 (1971)

J.N. OTT
Colour and light: their effect on
plants animals and people. *J. Biosoc.
Res.* 7(1): 1985

R. J. PELLEGRINI, A. G.
SCHAUSS et al
Leg strength as a function of expo-
sure to visual stimuli of different
hues. *Bulletin of the Psychonomic
Society* 16(2): 111-112 (1980)

J.B. PHILLIPS, S.C. BORLAND
Behavioural evidence for the use of
a light-dependent magnetoreception
mechanism by a vertebrate. *Nature*
1992, v359, p142-144

F.S. PRATO, M. KAVALIERS
Modulatory effects of light on nitric
oxide associated inhibitory effects of
extremely low frequency magnetic
fields on opioid-induced analgesia in
the land snail. *Bioelectromagnetics
Society* June 1998c

RUSSEL J. REITER
Effects of Light and stress on Pineal
Function in *ELF EM Fields: the question of Cancer*, Wilson, Stevens et al
(eds.) Battelle Press, Ohio, 1990

N.E. ROSENTHAL et al
Seasonal Affective Disorder: a
description of the syndrome and
preliminary findings with light
therapy. *Arch. Genl. Psychiatr.* 41: 72-
80 (1984)

N.E. ROSENTHAL, T.A. WEHR
Seasonal Affective Disorders.
Psychiatr. Ann. 17(10): 670-674
(October 1987)

A.G. SCHAUSS
The physiological effect of colour
on the suppression of human aggression: research on Baker-Miller pink.
Intl. J. Biosoc. Res. 72: 55-64 (1982)

M. SHODELL
The Curative light. *Science* pp47-51,
April 1982

B. SPIRE, D. DORMONT et al
Inactivation of LAV by heat, Gamma
Rays, and UV Light. *Lancet*, p.188,
January (1985)

S.J. WEBB
Genetic continuity and metabolic
regulation as seen by the effects of
various microwave and black light
frequencies on these phenomena.
Ann. NY. Acad. Sci. 247:327-351
(1975)

S.J. WEBB
Synthesis of DNA by specific frequencies. *Ann. N.Y. Acad. Sci.* 247: 327 (1975)

S.J. WEBB
Turning cancer cells to normal with microwaves. *Int J. of Quant. Chem. Quant. Biol. 1 Symp.* 1, 245-251

S.J. WEBB
The crystal properties of living cells as seen by millimeter micro-waves and raman spectroscopy. *Living State II* Pages 367-403)

P. WHITING
Improvements in reading and other skills using Irlen coloured lenses. *Austral. J. Remed. Educ.* 20: 13-15 (1987)

A.J. WICKINS, I. NIMROD-SMITH et al
Fluorescent lighting, Headaches, and eye strain. *Proc. Natl. Lighting Conference* (1988)

W. WILTSCHKO, H. MUNROLL, H. FORD, R. WILTSCHKO
Red light disrupts magnetic orientation of migratory birds. *Nature* 1993, v364, p525-527

H. WOHLFARTH
Psychological evaluation of experiments to assess the effects of colour stimuli upon the autonomic nervous system. *Excerpta Med. Neurol. Psychiatr.* 2 (4) 1958

R.J. WURTMAN, J. AXELROD
Melatonin synthesis in the pineal gland: effect of light mediated by the sympathetic nervous system. *Science* 147: 1328-1330 (1964)

S. YOUNG, P. BOLTON et al.
Macrophage responsiveness to light therapy. *Lasers In Surg. & Med.* 9: 497-505 (1989)

Resources

For national calls in UK or USA, dial the number listed here. From UK or the rest of the world to USA, dial 001 plus the number listed. From USA to UK, dial 00 44 and omit the first 0 of the number listed. For countries other than UK and USA, dial the number listed.

BICOM Therapy

Regumed
Lochamer Schlag 5a
D-82166 Gräfelfing, Germany
Telephone: 00 49 89 854 6101
Fax: 00 49 89 854 6103
Email: info@regumed.de
Website: www.regumed.com

West London BICOM Therapy and Osteopathy Centre
101 Netheravon Road South
London W4 2PZ, UK
Telephone: 020 8747 1766
Email: bicom.westlondon@gmx.net
Website:
www.bicom2000.freeserve.co.uk

Bioelectromagnetics

Coghill Research Laboratories
Lower Race
Pontypool
Gwent NP4 5UH, Wales, UK
Telephone: 01495 752122
Fax: 01495 769882
Email: enquiries@mag-lab.com
Website:www.cogreslab.demon.co.uk

Biolumanetics

Patrick Richards
4212 Oak Forest Court
Grand Rapids
Michigan 49549, USA
Telephone: 616 956 00523
Email: pricha4212@AOL.com
Website: www.biolumanetics.com

Thrity Engineer
199 Mortlake Road
Kew
Surrey TW9 4EWß, UK
Telephone: 020 8878 6693
Fax: 020 8404 2953
Website:
www.biolumaneticsat3s.com

Bioptron

Glowing Health Ltd
Jaysforde House
College Road
Newton Abbot
Devon TQ12 1EF, UK
Telephone: 01626 336 337
Fax: 01626 336 002
Email: glowingh@globalnet.co.uk
Website: www.glowingh.co.uk

Zepter International
USA Inc.
8400 River Road
North Bergen,
New Jersey 07047, USA
Telephone: 201 453 0637
Fax: 201 453 0641
Email: uros@zepter-usa.com
Website:
www.bioptron.com/pages/products.htm

Cocrysto torch

Also Eye Healing Lamp, Theo Gimbel's colour therapy training, treatments, and associated products.
Hygeia Studios
Brook House
Avening, Tetbury
Gloucester GL8 8NS, UK
Telephone: 01453 832150
Fax: 01453 835757

Full-spectrum lights and lightboxes

DW Viewboxes Ltd
Freepost MK 1241
Granby
Milton Keynes MK1 1XA, UK
Telephone: 01908 642323
Fax: 01908 640164
Email: sales@dw-view.com
Website: www.dw-view.com
30-day trial period. 4-monthly payment scheme – rental or purchase.

National Light Hire Company
2b Hartwood Road
Southport
Merseyside PR9 9AA, UK
Telephone: 0800 074 1105/01704 530919
Fax: 01704 501363
Email: sadbox@aol.com
Website: www.sadbox.com
Independent advice. Purchase and rental of all major products and "try before you buy" scheme.

Outside In (Cambridge) Ltd
Freepost 1071SV
Cambridge CB3 7BR, UK
Telephone: 01954 211955
Fax: 01954 211956
Email: info@outsidein.co.uk
Website: ww.outsidein.co.uk
3-year guarantee. 21-day trial scheme. Many additional light therapy products.

Philips Domestic Appliances and Personal Care
Bright Light
34 Hanway Street
London W1P 9DE, UK
Telephone: 020 7636 3942
Fax: 020 7636 3945
Email:
nigel.passingham@infoplan.co.uk
30-day money-back guarantee

The SAD Lightbox Company Ltd
19 Lincoln Road
Cressex Business Park
High Wycombe
Buckinghamshire HP12 3FX, UK
Telephone: 01494 448727/01494 526051
Fax: 01494 527005
Email:
carolbarksfield@compuserve.com
Website: www.sad.uk.com
28-day money-back guarantee. Efficient repairs while you wait.

Sunbox Designs Ltd
37 Eastern Road
London N2 9LB, UK
Telephone: 020 8444 9218
Fax: 020 8292 1613
Email: info@sunbox.co.uk
Website: www.sunbox.co.uk
28-day money-back guarantee

Verilux, Inc. "The Healthy Lighting Company"
9 Viaduct Road
Stamford,
Connecticut 06907, USA
Telephone: 203 921 2430 x 105
Toll-Free telephone number: 800 786 6850
Fax: 203 921 2427
Email: lmorton@ergolight.com
Website: www.verilux.net

Irlen Method

The Irlen Centre, London
Irena Corsini
24 Lofting Road
London N1 1ET, UK
Telephone: 07957 644665

Iridology

Society of Iridologists
40 Stokewood Road
Bournemouth BH3 7NE
Dorset, UK
Telephone: 020 2529 793

Knott Technique

Now called UBI therapy. The original Knott technique is being re-developed by Professor Kira Samoilova, Head of the Photobiology Unit of the Institute of Cytology, Russian Academy of Medical Sciences, St Petersburg, Russia. For details in the UK contact:
Simon Best
Box 2039,
Shoreham, W Sussex BN43 5JD, UK
email simon.best@euphony.net

For details in the US contact:
Mr Zee Harpaz
5282 Park Place Circle
Boca Raton, Florida 33486, USA.
Tel:ephone: 561 338 9441.
Email: mailto:zee@world-trader.com>zee@world-trader.com
Mr Harpaz is currrently coordinating the promotion and networking involved with making UBI more widely available in the USA. He also has names of doctors there and in other countries who are using UBI and he is the first point of contact for those wanting to know more.

LightMask

LightMask
PO Box 25632
London N10 3LL, UK
Telephone: 0870 5168143
Email: info@lightmask.com
Website: www.light-therapy.com
This website has excellent information and scientific articles on light therapy for treating conditions such as migraine, PMS, SAD, sleep disorders, and wounds.

Lux Caduceus III

Whale Medical
PO Box 31
Seaton
Devon E12 2YB, UK
Telephone: 01297 24288
Email:info@whalemedical.com
Website: whalemedical.com

Monocrom Light Dome

Thrity Engineer
199 Mortlake Road
Kew
Surrey TW9 4EWß, UK
Telephone/Fax: 020 8878 6693
Website:
www.lifeenhancementsystems.com

Karl Ryberg
Monocrom
Bergsgatan 53
112-31 Stockholm, Sweden
Telephone: 00 46 8 6500077
Email: karl@monocrom.se
Website: www.monocrom.se

Photobiology

*The European Society for Photobiology is
located at:*
Website: www.pol-europe.net

The American society for
Photobiology:
Website:www.kumc.edu/POL/ASP_
Home/asp_bro2.html

Photodynamic therapy

Laser Medical Research Foundation
Director: James S. McCaughan Jr.,
MD, FACS, FCCP, FASLMS, BS
Chem. Eng.
323 E. Town St, Columbus
Ohio 43215, USA
Telephone: 614 221 2643
Fax: 614 221 0149
Email: lasermed@iwaynet.net

*A brief description of photodynamic ther-
apy can also be found at the Cancer
Treatments Center of America (CTCA)*
Website:www.cancercenter.com/
home/2/39/169

Pip Scanner and Electro-crystal Therapy

Harry Oldfield Clinic and School of
Electro-Crystal Therapy
117 Long Drive, Ruislip
Middlesex HA4 0HL, UK
Website: www.electrocrystal.com

Seasonal Affective Disorder (SAD)

SAD Association
PO Box 989
Steyning
Sussex BN44 3HG, UK
Website: www.sada.org.uk
*Please send stamped addressed envelope
for free leaflet, or £5 for a comprehensive
information pack. Can supply information on UK light box hire schemes and
on specialist National Health SAD clinics in the UK.*

For general info on SAD practitioners:
Society for Light Treatment and
Biological Rhythms (SLTBR)
842 Howard Avenue
New Haven
Connecticut 06519, USA
Fax 203 764 4324
Email: sltbr@yale.edu
Website: www.sltbr.org

Syntonics

Aspen Center for Energy Medicine
PO Box 4058
Aspen
Colorado 81612-4058, USA
Telephone: 1800 576 8038

Tubular skylights

Natralux Ltd
Unit 7 Milburn Road
Westbourne, Bournemouth
Dorset BH4 9HJ, UK
Telephone: 01202 760777
Fax: 01202 768277
Email: sales@natralux.co.uk
Website: www.natralux.co.uk

Solatube
2210 Oak Ridge Way
Vista
California 92083, USA
Telephone: 888 476 5288
Fax: 760 599 3099
Website: www.solatube.com

Solatube Europe Ltd
51 Newport Road
Woburn Sands
Milton Keynes MK17 8UQ, UK
Telephone: 01908 585 840
Fax: 01908 585841
Email: sgme@solaglobal.com
Website: www.solatube.com

Index

A

acne 94, 137, 142
ACTH (adrenocorticotrophic hormone) 106
acupuncture 138
adenosine diphosphate (ADP) 142
adenosine triphosphate (ATP) 142, 143
Aluminium Spectro Chrome 115
Andrade, E.N. da C. 80
anemia 94
The Angel Standing in the Sun (Turner) 15
animals 48-9, 52, 65, 104, 105, 111
antibiotics 94, 132
antidepressants 57
antioxidants 53, 101
Apollo 28-9
appendicitis 128
Appleton Laboratory 36
Aristotle 68, 78
arteriosclerosis 94
arthritis 57, 94, 146
asthma 57, 94, 97, 115
atoms 68, 76, 80
attention span *see* concentration
auras
    and light therapy 128-32
    see also endogenous fields
aurora australis 76
aurora borealis 76
Aztecs 31

B

Baal 28
Babbit, Edwin 112
back pain 139
bacteria 91, 92-4, 129, 132
Becker, Robert 65
Benoit, J. 111
Best, Simon 65
betablockers 56
BICOM 137, 138
Biofeedback imaging 140
Biolumanetics 139, 140
Bioptron 136-7
bioresonance therapy (BRT) 137
Blake, William 84
blood 57, 114, 117, 129-30, 143
blood pressure 94, 97, 115, 116

Blue and Red Lights (Pancoast) 112
Blunt, Thomas 92, 93, 132
Bohr, Niels 78
brain 57, 82, 84, 128, 144
breast lumps 146
Bronze Age 35
Brügemann, Hans 138
Brügemann Institute 137
Buddha and Buddhism 18-20, 41
burns 94

C

caffeine 54, 56
calcium 92, 94, 96
calendars 10, 30, 34, 36
cancer 57, 91, 96, 127, 128, 132, 136, 142-4
    skin 97, 100, 105
Carnac 34
Castle Rigg, Cumbria 34
cataracts *see* eyes
cellulite 149
Cerebellum Multifunction Medical Instrument (CMMI) 137
CFCs (chorofluorocarbons) 97
chakras 117, 146
Chartres Cathedral 9
children 86, 103, 105, 115, 116
chlorophyll 58, 142
chloroplasts 104
chocolate 56
cholecalciferol 92
cholesterol 97
Christianity 16, 24-5
Clavelina lepadiformis (lightbulb tunicates) 78
CoCrysto torch 146
cola 56
colitis 94, 146
College of Syntonic Optometry 131
Collis, John Stewart 83
colour 70, 71, 74, 111-12, 117
colour therapy 112-15, 131
Columbia University, NY 96
communications 15, 88-9
concentration (attention span) 105, 108, 116
cortisol 105
cot deaths 61
County Meath, Ireland 35
La Cure du Soleil (Rollier) 93
cystitis 94, 146

D

Dante 16
De Iride (Theodoric) 74
Dee, John 88
Democritus 68
depression 54, 57, 60, 61, 104, 105, 108, 140
    see also SAD
Descartes, René, 50, 70, 71, 74
DHE (Photofrin) 144
diet 101
Dinshah 114, 115
Divali 17
Donne, John 40
Dougherty, Thomas 143
Downes, Arthur 92, 93, 132
Duro-Test Corporation 105

E

eclipses 46–7
eczema 94, 142, 146
Egypt 29-30, 34, 35
Einstein, Albert 76, 78, 79
electrical energy 78, 116, 127, 128, 142
electromagnetic energy 11, 67, 75, 76, 80, 85, 116, 129
electrons 76, 79, 82-3, 86, 142
ELF fields 94, 96, 116
endogenous fields 11, 116-17, 127, 128-30
energy 11, 76, 78, 79, 80, 139
    and the body 138, 140, 142
Engineer, Thrity 140
epilepsy 57, 128
ergocalciferol 92
Ertel, H. 115
Espiritu, Rachelle 54
Euler, Leonard 71
Exploring the Spectrum (film) 104
Eye Healing Lamp 146
eyes 67, 84-5, 89, 105, 115, 136
    cataracts 97, 115, 146
    colour therapy 115, 117
    light therapy 131, 132, 146
    see also glasses

F

family dynamics 139
Faraday, Michael 75
fatigue 104, 105, 108

Fenyo, Marta 136
fibre optics 15, 86, 89, 144
Finsen, Niels 92
fire 11, 20
Fizeau, H.L. 83
Flammarion, C. 112
floral clock 44–5
fluorescent lighting 58, 86, 91, 104,
   105-6, 116
Food and Drug Administration
   (FDA) 132
fractals 79
fractures 96
Fraunhofer lines 114
free radicals 53, 142
Freud, Sigmund 115

G

gamma rays 130
geese, Canada 49
Gerber, Richard 117
germination 65
Ghadiali, Dinshah P. *see* Dinshah
Gimbel, Theo 112, 146
Giotto 38
glasses 101, 105, 116, 128
glaucoma 115, 146
glutamate 52
glycolysis 142
glycoproteins 143
gout 94
gynecological conditions 144

H

haloes 16, 20, 25, 26
Hammersmith Hospital, London 130
Hancock, Virgil 132
Hannukah 21
Hanovia UV lamp 132
Harman, Denman 53
hay fever 115
headaches 104, 105, 110, 136
heart 57, 82, 97, 114, 115, 117
Heisenberg, Werner 78
heliotherapy 92-7
Helmholtz, Hermann 89
hemo-irradiation 86, 91, 132, 136
hemorrhoids 137
hepatitis 128
herpes simplex 137
Hieronymus, T. Galen 58

Hinduism 16-17
Hippocampus Research Institute,
Budapest 137
Hoffman, Roger 52
Hollwich, Fritz 86, 105
Hopkins, Gerard Manley 16, 120
hormones 97, 105
The Human Atmosphere (Kilner)
   128
Huygens, Christiaan 71
Hygeia College of Colour Therapy
   112
hyperactivity 86, 105, 116
hypersomnia 108
hypertension 97, 117

I

immune system responses 136
Incas 10, 35
infection 91
infrared radiation 80, 148
injuries *see* trauma
ionosphere 65, 76, 91, 96
Irlen, Helen 116
irritability 105, 108
Islam 26

J

Jalalu'l-Din Rumi 26
jaundice 17, 132
jet lag 44, 57, 109
"Jet Lag Visor" 105
Judaism 21, 24, 26
Jupiter (planet) 82

K

Kato (biologist) 111
Kilner, Walter 128
Kirchhoff, G.B. 138
Knott, Emmitt 132
Kollerstrom, Nick 65
Kramers, H.A. 78
Kyoto University 111

L

Laser Biology Institute, Moscow 140
lasers 15, 144
Lednyiczky, Gabor 137
Leeds General Infirmary 92

Leucippus 68
Lewy, Alfred 53
Leysin clinic 93
Liberman, Jacob 97, 127, 149
libido, loss of 108
Light: Medicine of the Future
   (Liberman) 97, 149
light
   and the body 11, 84, 85, 86, 88
   cycles 43-4
   in the home 120, 122-4
   nature of 11, 15, 67, 70, 75-8, 80
   polarized 136, 137
   speed 71, 82-3, 89
   spiritual 15, 16
light boxes 108, 109, 110
light therapy 11, 53, 94, 109, 110,
   127, 149
   and auras 128-32
lighting
   full spectrum 104-10, 115, 116,
   136
   interior design 120, 122-4
LightMask 130
lightning 82
Linnaeus, Carolus 44
London School of Hygiene and
   Tropical Medicine 86
Lucretius 68
Luminator 139, 140
lunar cycles 64-5
lupus vulgaris 92
Lux Caduceus III 146
lymphocytes 116, 129, 130

M

mastitis 137
al-Masudi 26
matter 79, 80
Matthaus the Elder 21
Maxwell, James Clerk 75, 79, 82-3
Maya 30, 31, 35
meditation 40-1
melanoma 57, 100, 101
melatonin 50-7, 60, 88, 105, 108, 111
mental disorders 117, 128
Mexico 31, 34, 35
migraine 130, 131, 139
migration 48–9
Minerals Metabolism Unit, Leeds
   General Infirmary 92
moles 100

Moloch 28
Monet, Claude 38
Monocrom Light Dome 140
mood 108, 111
moon 17, 18, 20, 30, 46, 64–5
"moonbeam telegraph" 88
Moses 21
MRSA (methycillin-resistant
    Staphylococcus aureus) 91
Muhammad 26
Müller, Max 16
mythology 11, 28–33

N

NASA 105
National Institute of Radiobiology,
    Budapest 136
National Radiological Protection
    Board (NRPB) 96, 97
Native Americans 32
negative ions 34–5, 41
nervous system 112
New Natural House Book (Pearson)
    120
Newgrange 34, 35
Newlyn Gallery, Cornwall 38
Newton, Isaac 70, 71
Noton, David 130
NSAIDS (non-steroidal anti-
    inflammatory drugs) 56

O

Oishi (biologist) 111
Oldfield, Harry 128
Oppenheimer, Robert 17
The Opticks (Newton) 70
osteomalacia 92
osteoporosis 94
Ott, John 101, 104, 105
Otto, Rudolph 16
oxidative phosphorylation 142
oxygen 53, 93, 137, 142, 143
ozone layer 97

P

pain 57, 114
Pancoast, Seth 112
Paradiso (Dante) 16
Parry, Barbara 52
particles 68, 71, 76, 78
Paterson lamp 144–5

PDT (photodynamic therapy) 142–5
Pearson, David 120, 122
phobias 140
Phoenicians 28
photobiology 92
photodynamic therapy (PDT) 142–5
Photofrin (DHE) 144
photon platinum 148, 149
photons 76, 78, 88
photosynthesis 57
phototherapy 132–5
Photron 131
Pi in the Sky (Poynder) 35
pineal gland 50, 52, 56, 84, 88, 109,
    111
Pirsig, Robert 15
Planck, Max 76
plants 43, 44, 48–9, 65, 105, 111–12
Pleasanton, A.J. 111
Pliny the Elder 65
pneumonia 115
Polycontrast Interference
    Photography (PIP) 128
porphyrins 142, 143, 144
positive ions 64
Pourbus, Pieter 25
Poynder, Michael 35
premenstrual syndrome (PMS) 52,
    109, 130, 131
The Principles of Light and Colour
    (Babbit) 112
psoriasis 97, 137, 146
Ptolemy, Claudius 65
pyramids 34, 35

R

radiation 76, 79, 80, 94, 130, 146
radio waves 76, 89
rainbows 71–4
Rao, M.L. 54
Re 29–30
Reiter, Russel 50, 52
religion 10, 15–32
reproductive function 111, 114
rhodopsin 88
rhythms
    brain 82, 128
    circadian 43, 44, 60, 109
    light 43, 48–9
Richards, Patrick 139
rickets 92
Rife, Royle 85
Roemer, Ole Christian 82, 83

Rollier, Auguste 93, 94
Rosenthal, Norman E. 105
Roswell Park Memorial Institute
    143
Royal Society, London 70
Rudolf II, Emperor 88
Russian Academy of Sciences 132
Ryberg, Karl 140

S

SAD (Seasonal Affective Disorder)
    57, 104–10, 140
Sahley, Bill 56
Sam, Catherine 115
Samoilova, Kira 132
Seasonal Affective Disorder (SAD)
    57, 104–10, 140
septic conditions 115, 132
serotonin 53, 54, 64
Shekhinah 21, 24
signal transduction 94
Sixty Minutes (Irlen) 116
skin 85, 102
    diseases 92, 97, 100, 105, 142, 144
    types 102
Slater, John 78
sleep 57, 108, 110
Sohal, Rajindar 53
solarized water 112
solitrol 97
spectacles *see* glasses
spectral emission lines (Fraunhofer
    lines) 114
*Spectro-Chrome Metry
    Encyclopaedia* (Dinshah) 114
spectrum 70, 74, 91
Spitler, Harry Riley 131
sprains 115
stained glass 9, 10, 21–3
Stephenson, John 136
stomach 117, 132
Stonehenge 10, 34, 35, 36
stress 57, 108, 131, 140
subatomic particles *see* electrons
Sufism 26
Sun
    calendars 34–6
    religion 10, 15–18, 20, 28–32
sunbeds 100, 109
sunburn 100–1, 102–3
sunflower 48
sunglasses 101, 105
sunlight

exposure 96, 100-4
   therapy 57, 91, 92
sunscreens 101, 103
sunspots 36
suprachiasmatic nuclei (SCN) 52, 84
syntonics 131, 132

T

Tao Tsang 52
Teotihuacan 34
Theodoric 71, 74
Thomson, Sir Joseph John 83
"*Transfiguration on Mount Tabor*"
   (Pourbus) 25
trauma 114, 115, 137
tryptophan 54, 56
tuberculosis 92, 93, 94
Turner, J.M.W. 15
Turrell, James 38

U

ulcers 57, 115, 132, 136
ultraviolet light 80, 85, 86, 91, 92-7,
   100, 109, 112, 129, 130

V

VDUs 136
Vermeer 38
Virtual Daylight 136
The Vision of Glory (Collis) 83
Vitale, Barbara Meister 116
VitaLite 105
vitamin D
   deficiency 94, 96
   and sunlight 40, 61, 91, 92, 97, 100
   and sunscreens 101
VRIC (Visual Reference of Image
   Coherence) 139

W

weight loss 97
Whale, Jon 146
Wohlfarth, Harry 115
Wu Li 78, 79

X Y

X-rays 76, 130
Yacomicqui 31
Young, Thomas 75, 76

Z

*Zen and the Art of Motorcycle
   Maintenance* (Pirsig) 15
Zoroastrianism 20, 26
Zukav, Gary 78
Zunis 35

Author's acknowledgements

I would like to acknowledge the contribution of my dear wife Tamara, who reinforced my own initially sceptical attitude about this subject, and thereby honed away some of the less supportable claims being made. I would never have attempted this book unless encouraged by Pip Morgan of Gaia, and when the going got tough in unfamiliar waters the help I received from Jinny Johnson and Sara Mathews was invaluable. I found all those already familiar with aspects of light therapy always helpful in their explanations, and I have realized that the vastness of the subject I have tackled will inevitably mean revisiting the topic in more depth some day.

Publisher's acknowledgements

Gaia Books would like to thank Helena Petre for all her invaluable help with the text and for compiling the list of resources, James Harpur for his work and advice on the role of light in religions, Gwen Rigby for proof-reading, Elizabeth Wiggans for compiling the index, Matt Moate for design assistance and Thrity Engineer for her assistance on the subject of light therapy and for allowing the team to sample the healing effects of the Monocrom Light Dome.

Photographic credits

Title Page, Robert Harding Picture Library; Contents page, Britistock-Ifa; 8, Sonia Halliday Photographs; 12-13, Photodisc; 14, ©Tate Gallery; 16, Photodisc; 17, Hutchison Library/ Goycolea; 18, AKG London/Erich 19, Photodisc; 20, Hutchison Library/Emile S.; 21, AKG London; 22-23, Photodisc; 24, AKG London; 25, AKG London/Erich Lessing; 27, Photodisc; 28, AKG London/Erich Lessing; 30-37, Robert Harding Picture Library; 39, Steve Tanner; 41, Robert Harding Picture Library; 42-44, Photodisc; 46, Science Photo Library/Jean-Loup Charmet; 47, Science Photo Library/David Nunuk; 48-49B, Britstock-Ifa/Alaska Stock; 48, Photodisc; 50, Gaia; 51, Science Photo Library/Dr Jeremy Burgess; 52-55, Robert Harding Picture Library; 59, Britstock-Ifa/Bernd Ducke; 60-1, Britstock-Ifa/ibt; 62-3, Britstock-Ifa/H.Schmidbauer; 64, Photodisc; 66, Science Photo Library/James L. Amos, Peter Arnold Inc.; 69, Britstock-Ifa/Grafenhain; 71, Photodisc; 72-3, Robert Harding Picture Library; 75, Science Photo Library/Dr Jeremy Burgess; 76, Photodisc; 77, Science Photo Library/B & C Alexander; 78, Science Photo Library/George Gornacz; 79, Gaia; 81, Robert Harding Picture Library; 82-83, Photodisc; 87, Science Photo Library/Quest; 88 R, C, L, Photodisc; 88-9, Robert Harding Picture Library; 89 L,C,R, Photodisc; 90, Photodisc; 93, AKG London; 95, Photodisc; 97, Gaia; 98-9, Britstock-Ifa; 100, Still Pictures/Mark Edwards; 102-3, Britstock-Ifa/Bernd Ducke; 105, Science Photo Library/Hank Morgan; 107, Science Photo Library/Hank Morgan; 109, Outside In; 113, Eduardo Munoz/The Interior Archive (Designer: Nacho Vicens); 118-19, Warren du Preez; 121, Fritz von der Schulenburg/The Interior Archive; 122, Herbert Ypma/The Interior Archive (Architect: Javier Sordo); 125, Tim Clinch/The Interior Archive (Owner: Handelsmann); 126-7, Warren du Preez; 128, Photo: Harry Oldfield, courtesy of Carrie Haines; 130, LightMask; 133, Science Photo Library/Martin Dohrn; 134-35, Science Photo Library/BSIP Astier; 136, Glowing Health/Bioptron; 139, Thrity Engineer, courtesy of 3S; 140-41 Thrity Engineer, courtesy of Life Enhancement Systems; 142, Science Photo Library/John Durham; 143, Science Photo Library/Professors P.M.Motta & S. Correr; 145, Science Photo Library/David Parker; 146-7, Whale Medical/ www.whalemedical.com; 148-49, Phil O'Connor; 150, Britstock-Ifa.